A KEY

To the Knowledge and Use of the

BOOK OF COMMON PRAYER

By J. H. BLUNT, M.A.

EDITOR OF "THE DICTIONARY OF THEOLOGY." "THE ANNOTATED
BOOK OF COMMON PRAYER"
AUTHOR OF "HOUSEHOLD THEOLOGY," &c. &c

*" I will pray with the spirit, and I will pray with the understanding also:
I will sing with the spirit, and I will sing with the understanding also."*
1 COR. xiv. 15

RIVINGTONS

London, Oxford, and Cambridge

1871

[*New Edition*]

Contents

CHAPTER I

The History of the Prayer Book

" Thus saith the LORD, *Stand ye in the ways, and see, and ask for the old paths, where is the good way, and walk therein, and ye shall find rest for your souls."*—JER. vi.

THE English Book of Common Prayer is chiefly derived from the Latin "Breviary," "Missal," and "Manual," which were used in England for many centuries before the Reformation. The Pre-Reformation "Breviary" contained the Daily Services Service-books. (including the Lessons) ; the " Missal " contained the Service for the Holy Communion (including the Epistles and Gospels) ; and the " Manual " contained the Offices for Baptism, the Visitation of the Sick, Burial, &c.

These ancient Prayer Books of the Church of England had their origin in Apostolic times, Their Primitive having gradually grown up out of Services origin. which were brought to France by Apostolic missionaries, who came from Ephesus and Smyrna. The Services thus transplanted from the East were used in common by the Churches of France, Spain, and England ; but additions peculiar to How differing each country gradually gathered around Liturgies arose.

B

the original formularies, and in course of time the devotional system of each became so far different from
that of the others as to be a *national* rite, though bearing abundant marks of relationship to the rest. Just
as Frenchmen, Spaniards, and Englishmen differ from
each other in some respects, and yet have the common
characteristics of the European family of nations so
their ancient devotional systems plainly come from the
same original stock, though differing in many particular features.[1]

But by far the greater proportion of the Services of
the Church is (and always has been) taken from the
Psalms and other portions of Holy Scripture.

§ 1. *The Latin originals of the Prayer Book.*

THE Eastern missionaries, St. Pothinus and others,
who brought over to France the devotional forms of
the Eastern Church, brought them in the Greek language ; and Greek words (such as *Kyrie Eleëson*)
were retained in the Latin services in reverent memory
of the ancient liturgical language, as the Latin head-
ings of the Psalms and Canticles are retained in our
Greek super- English Prayer Book. But as Latin was
seded by Latin the universal language of the Roman Empire in Europe, the services were soon translated out of
Greek into Latin ; and they were used in the latter
tongue in England as well as elsewhere until the

---

[1] The Roman Breviary, &c., was not introduced into
England until about a century and a half ago, when the
priests of the Roman sect were chiefly Jesuits, and so bound
to use it. It was never used therefore in the Church of
England. Nor was it generally used in France until after
the Revolution.

English language became compacted out of Saxon, French, and Latin into its modern form[2].

The Service Books which were in use Sarum and before the Conquest were revised by St. other "Uses" Osmund, Bishop of Salisbury, and his revision, the ancient "Sarum Use" mentioned in the Preface to the Prayer Book, was adopted in the Diocese of Salisbury in the year 1085. Other dioceses had similar Service Books of their own, known as the "York Use," the "Hereford Use," the "Lincoln Use," &c.; but the "Sarum Use" was extensively adopted throughout the South of England, in Durham, in some parts of Scotland, and even on the Continent; and it was the principal source from which the Prayer Book "according to the use of the Church of England" was taken in the sixteenth century.

§ 2. *Early English Prayers, &c.*

WHILE the public Services of the Church of England were said chiefly in Latin, persons who could read had Prayer Books called "Primers," in which Primers what a large portion of the Psalms and the they were Prayers were translated, and arranged in Services similar to those which were used in Latin at the Cathedrals and large Monastic or Collegiate Churches. This

[2] French, or "Norman French," was the language used in this country by educated persons until the end of the fourteenth century. Latin was the official language, and was very generally understood. Saxon, or "Anglo-Saxon," was in a continual state of change until the time of Chaucer (A.D 1328—1400), and about his time it began to be amalgamated with French and Latin forms of words into our present national language. Mediæval English is represented at the present day by what is called "Broad Scotch."

" Primer " or Layman's Prayer Book, is found in Anglo-
Saxon of a very early period, and in English of the
fourteenth century. It was revised and republished in
the reigns of Henry VIII., Edward VI., Queen Mary,
and Queen Elizabeth : and is the basis of " Cosin's
Devotions," a book still used by many. Some portions
Parts of Divine Service in English. of the Sunday Services were also in English, as the Exhortation and Confession
in the Communion Service, and the " Bid-
ding of Bedes " (or prayers), the latter of which was the
popular Sunday Service of mediæval times. There
were also interlined translations of the Litany and the
Psalms, some of which still remain, nearly 1000 years
old. The Creeds, the Lord's Prayer, and the Ten
Commandments were also very frequently recited in
English, and expounded from the pulpit ; and portions
of the " Occasional Offices " were used in the mother
tongue.

The following few specimens will illustrate this use
of English in ancient days, but there is not room here
to print any number of such illustrations :—

Evening Prayer.

"Oure fadir, that art in heuenes, halewid be thi name :
thy rewme come to thee · be thi wille do
Primer, A D. 1400. as in heuene and in erthe : oure eche daies
breed gyue us to day: and forgyue us our dettise,
as and we forgeuen to oure dettouris : and ne lede us into
temptacioun : but delyuere us fro yuel. So be it.

     Lord, thou schalt opyne myn lippis.
      And my mouth schal schewe thi prisynge.
     God, take heede to myn helpe.
     Lord, hige thee to help me.

"Glorie be to the fadir and to the sone and to the holy
goost :

" As it was in the begynnyng and now and euer and in to the worldis of worldis. So be it.

God make us saaf.

Alleluia.

*   *   *   *   *   *

"I bileue in god, fadir almygti, makere of heuene and of erthe : and in iesu crist the sone of him, oure lord, oon alone : which is conceyued of the hooli gost : born of marie maiden : suffride passioun undir pounce pilat : crucified, deed, and biried : he went doun to hellis : the thridde day he roos agen fro deede : he steig to heuenes : he sittith on the rigt syde of god the fadir almygti : thenns he is to come for to deme the quyke and deede. I beleue in the hooli goost : feith of hooli chirche : communynge of seyntis : forgyuenesse of synnes · agenrisyng of fleish, and euerlastynge lyf. So be it.

" Preie we.

" Lord, haue merci on us.
Crist, haue merci on us.
Lord, haue merci on us.

*   *   *   *   *   *

"Lord, sheu to us thi merci,
And geue to us thi saluacioun.

*   *   *   *   *   *

" Lord, gyue pees in oure daies, for ther is noon othir that shal fygte for us, but thou O lord oure god.

Preie we.   For the pees.

" God of whom ben hooli desiris, rigt councels and iust werkis : gyue to thi seruantis pees that the world may not geue, that in our hertis gouun to thi commandementis, and the drede of enemys putt awei, oure tymes be pesible thurgh thi defendyng. Bi oure lord iesu crist, thi sone, that with thee lyueth and regneth in the unitie of the hooli goost god, bi all worldis of worldis. So be it.

"God, that taughtist the hertis of thi feithful seruantis bi the lightnynge of the hooli goost : graunte us to sauore rigtful thingis in the same goost, and to be ioiful euermore of his counfort. Bi crist our lorde. So be it.

*   *   *   *   *   *

" Almyghti god, euerlastynge, that aloone doost many

wondres, schewe the spirit of heelful grace upon bisschopes thi seruantis, and upon alle the congregacion betake to hem: and gheete in the dewe of thi blessynge that thei plese euermore to the in trouthe. Bi crist oure lord. So be it."

Holy Communion.

"Good men and women, y charge yow by the Auctoryte of holy churche, that no man nother woman that this day proposyth here to be comenyd [*communicated*] that he go note to Godds bord, lase than he byleue stedfastlych, that the sacrament that he ys avysyd here to reseue, that yt ys Godds body flesche and blode, yn the forme of bred ; & that (*which*) he receyvythe afterward, ys no thyng ells but wyne & water, for to clense yowr mowthys of the holy sacrament. Furthermor, y charge yow that no man nother woman go to Godds borde lase than he be of ys synnys clen confessyd, & for hem contryte ; that ys to sey hauyng sorow yn yowr herts, for yowre synnys. Furthermore, I charge yow yf ther be eny man or woman, that beryth yn his herte eny wrothe or rancor to eny of his evencristen [*fellow-Christian*] that he be not ther howselyd, ther to the tyme that he be with hym yn perfyte love & cheryte, for ho so [*whoso*] beryth wrethe or evyll wyll yn herte, to eny of hys evencristen, he ys note worthy hys God to receyue ; and yf he do, he reseyvythe his dampnacyon, where he schuld recyue his saluacion. Furthermore, y charge yow that none of yow go to Godds borde to day, lasse than he be yn full wyll & purpose for to sese and to withstond the deds of syn. For who proposyth now to contynue yn syn ayene after hys holy tyme he is note worthy to receyue his God ; & yf he do hyt ys to hym grete perell. Further-more I charge all strangers bothe men and women, that none of yow go to godds borde, yn to tyme that ye haue spoke with me, other [*or*] with myn asynys. Furthermore, y charge yow bothe men and women that havythe servants, that ye takythe hede that they be well y gouernyd yn takyng of mets & drynks, for the perell that may be fall, thorow forfeytyng of mets & drynks . . . . Also ye shall knell adown apon yowr kneys, seyying after me, y cry God mercy, and our lady seynt mary, & all the holy company of hevyn, & my gostelyche fadyr, of all the trespasse of syn that y have don, in thowte, word, other [*or*] yn dede, from the tyme that y

Missal, about A.D. 1350—1400.

was bore, yn to this tyme; that ys to say in Pryde, Envy, Wrethe, Slowthe, Covetyse, Gloteny, & Lechery. The v. Commawndements, dyuerse tymys y broke. The werks of mercy note y fulfyllyd. My v. wytts mysse spend, *etc.*"

Holy Matrimony.

"Lo breyren and sustren her we beon comyn to gedre in ye worsschip of god and his holy seintes in ye face of holy chirche to joynen to gedre Manual, yuse tweyne bodies yat heynforward yei beon A.D. 1408[3]. body in ye beleue and in ye lawe of god for te deserven everlastynge lyf wat so yei hau don here byfore. Wherfore i charge you on holy chirche by half alle yt here bes yat gif eni mon or womman knowen eny obstacle prevei or apert why yt ycy lawefully mowe nogt come to gedre in ye sacrament of holy churche sey ye now or neuer more.

  *   *   *   *   *   . - *

"Also I charge you both, and eyther be your selfe, as ye wyll answer before God at the Manual, about day of dome, that yf there be any thynge done 1350—1400. pryuely or openly, betwene your selfe : or that ye knowe any lawfull lettyng why that ye may not be wedded togyther at thys time : Say it nowe, or we do any more to this mater.

"*N.* Wilt thou haue this woman to thy wyfe : and loue her and kepe her in syknes and in helthe, and in all other degrese be to her as a husbande sholde be to his wyfe, and all other forsake for her : and holde thee only to her, to thy lyues ende? *Respondeat vir hoc modo :* I wyll.

"*N.* Wylt thou have this man to thy husbande, and to be buxum to him, serue him and kepe him in sykenes and in helthe : And in all other degrese be vnto hym as a wyfe should be to hir husbande, and all other to forsake for hym : and holde thee only to hym to thy lyues ende? *Respondeat mulier hoc modo :* I wyll.

"I *N.* take the *N.* to my weddyd wyf to haue and to holde fro thys day wafor beter, for worse, for rycher, for porer : in sykenesse and in helthe, tyl deth us departe yf

---

[3] This Manual (now in the British Museum) anciently belonged to the parish in which these pages are written.

holy chyrch wol it ordeyne and ther to I plycht the my
trouth.

"I *N.* take the *N.* to my weddyd husbonde to haue and
to holde fro thys day for bether, for wurs, for richer, for
porer, in sykenesse and hin elthe to be bonour and buxum
in bed and at bort : tyll deth us departe yf holy chyrche wol
it ordeyne : and ther to I plyche te my throute.

"With this rynge I wedde the, and with this gold and
silver I honoure the, and with this gyft I honoure the. In
nomine Patris : et Filii : et Spiritus Sancti. Amen."

The Visitation of the Sick.

"Brother, be ye gladde y^t ye shall dye in Chrysten beleve?
Re. Ye, syr.

"Knowe ye well y^t ye have not so well lyved as ye shulde?
Ye, syr.

"Haue ye wille to amende yow if ye had space to lyve?
Ye, syr.

"Beleve ye that o^r Lorde Christ Jhu goddys soon of
heaven was born of the blessyd vyrgyne ou^r ladie saynt Mary?
Ye, syr.

"Beleve ye that our Lorde Christ Jhu dyed vpon the
crosse to bye mans sowle upō the good firydaie? Ye, syr.

"Thancke ye him entierly therof? Ye, syr.

"Beleve ye y^t ye may not be saved but by his precious
death ? Ye, syr.

"Tunc dicat sacerdos.

"Therfor, Brother, while yor sowle is in yor bodye,
thancke ye god of his death, and haue ye hole truste, to be
saved, through his precyouse death, and thyncke ye on non
other worldely goode, but onely in Christe Jhus deathe,
and on his pytefull passyon, and saye after me, My swete
Lorde Christ Jhu, I put thy precyous passion betwene the
and my evill werke and betwene me and thy wrathe.

"Et dicat infirmus ter.

"In manus tuas Domine, etc   *Vel sic* —

"Lorde Christ Jhu, in to thy handes I betake my sowle
and as thow boughtest me, bodye and soule I betake to
the."

§ 3.—*The first complete English Prayer Book for Public Use.*

AFTER various reforms in the ancient Latin Service Books (between 1516 and 1541) it was at last determined that no more of them should be printed, but that English Services should be formed from them which should represent all their essential features, but yet be cast in a form more intelligible to and more useable by the people at large.

A Committee of Convocation was appointed in 1542 to undertake this work, but their labours were not allowed fully to see the light until the death of Henry VIII. <small>A.D. 1542. First steps.</small>

The old English Litany was, however, revised, and set forth for public use in its present form in 1544. Other Litanies or "Processions" were translated by Archbishop Cranmer, or under his direction ; but the King would not permit them to be used, nor any thing further to be done in altering the Services, beyond the reading of the Lessons in English, a practice that had been adopted for some time past. <small>A.D. 1544. The old English Litany revised.</small>

Immediately after the death of Henry VIII. the Clergy, however, began to urge forward the completion of the Prayer Book. On March 8th, 1547-8, an English Communion Service was issued as a supplement to the Latin one, for the use of the Laity, for the purpose of drawing them to more frequent Communion, and of administering both elements to them. <small>A.D. 1548. English Communion Service.</small>

The Prayer Book itself was completed by the Committee of Bishops and other clergy about seven months afterwards, <small>A.D. 1549. Complete Prayer Book.</small>

and was presented to Convocation by them at the end
of November, 1548. The Convocation sent it to the
King in Council, by whom it was laid before Parliament to be incorporated into an Act of Parliament,
the first Act of Uniformity [2nd & 3rd Edward VI.
ch. 1.]. This Act (including the Prayer Book, exactly
as it was sent up by Convocation), was passed at the
end of January, and enacted that the Prayer Book
should be taken into general use on the following
Whitsun Day, which was June 9th, 1549. It was
printed immediately, and published on March 7th,
1548-9, to give the clergy time to become familiar
with its contents. Many began to use it before Whitsun Day arrived, and when that solemn day came, the
English Order of Divine Service (which was declared
in the Act to have been composed under the influence
of the Holy Ghost) entirely superseded the ancient
Latin Services from which it had been formed

What changes   The principal changes which had been
had been made made (besides that of translation into
English) were

1. The condensation of seven daily services into
   Mattins and Evensong
2. The singing through of the Psalter every
   twenty-eight days, instead of every seven days.
3. The omission of all Lesson except those taken
   from Holy Scripture.
4. The omission of many Festival Services.

Substance of the   The other changes which were made
ancient services were mostly with the object of condensing
retained   lengthy offices, or of abolishing extrava-
gant modes of expression respecting the Blessed
Virgin Mary, and other saints. But most of what was
thus put away had been introduced into the Service

Books in comparatively recent times : and the claim
of the Reformers that they had retained, *in their substance*, the ancient services of the Church of England,
was in reality a just one.

§ 4. *The alteration of the first Prayer Book in deference to the Puritans.*

THE Book of Common Prayer thus completed was
at first received by all except a few foreigners who
had been too hospitably entertained by the English
Bishops, and by the self-willed Puritans, who always
did and always will object to Services which corre-
spond to the principles of the Church. Archbishop
Cranmer described these as "glorious and Cranmer's opin-
unquiet spirits which can like nothing but ion of the
that is after their own fancy ; and cease Puritans
not to make trouble when things be most quiet and in
good order. If such men," he added, "should be
heard, although the Book were made every year anew,
yet it should not lack faults in their opinion."

These unquiet spirits had the ear, how- A.D. 1552
ever, of Edward VI. and his uncle, the Their pressure
makes a revision
Duke of Somerset, the Protector (or Re- necessary
gent), neither of whom loved the Church or its principles and the power of the Crown was so enormous
during the rule of the Tudors, that the only way of
saving the Prayer Book from tyrannical destruction
was by the concession of some of the demands made
by the Puritans, with a boy-King and a profligate
Regent for their leaders.

The Prayer Book of 1549 was therefore "revised"
in 1552 ; but it had scarcely been printed for general

use before the death of Edward VI. and the accession

Prayer Book suppressed by law under Q Mary, 1553—8, of Queen Mary led to the restoration of the old Church system and the Latin Services. .The proper legal forms were used, in Parliament and elsewhere, for undoing the whole of the ten years' proceedings connected with the Prayer Book, and thus it ceased to have any legal existence, (after having been used for four years and a half,) in October, 1553.

and revised by law under Q Elizabeth, A D 1559, Shortly after Queen Elizabeth came to the throne [Nov. 17, 1558], the English Services were revived ; but to re-establish them on a legal footing, new Acts of Convocation and of Parliament had become necessary. It also became a question whether the Prayer Book should be revived in its original form, that of 1549, or in its altered shape, that of 1552. The Queen, Lord Burleigh, and those who wished to make the English Services comprehensive, and to connect them with the old Church of England, desired to restore the first ; but those of the Bishops and Clergy who had adopted Presbyterian customs and principles when abroad during the reign of Mary, considered the second Book more favourable to the novelties which they had learned. In the end, with some changes. the second Book was adopted, but with some important changes, which made it more like the first one again : especially as to definite recognition of those sacramental principles which the Puritans endeavoured, but always without success, to drive out of the Church

The Book, thus re-published under the authority of Church and State as before, remained in use without any further changes until it was suppressed at the time of the great Rebellion. The Puritans were unceasingly

assailing it all that time; and when James I. came to
the throne he summoned a Conference of
Church Divines and Puritans, at Hampton Court, with the view of discussing
the differences between them, and coming to a better
understanding. But the arrogant demands of the
Puritans so disgusted the King that after three days
he dissolved the Conference, and only a few small
verbal alterations were made in the Prayer Book. The
great Lord Bacon (himself almost a Puritan) painted
the characteristics of these wrong-headed controver-
sialists with a happy stroke of witty truth, when he
said : "They lacked but two things, the one being
learning, and the other *love*."

In the reign of Charles I. the Scottish
Bishops endeavoured to introduce the
English Prayer Book into Scotland, but
without success. They, however, reviewed it very
carefully, made many alterations, and submitted their
revised Book to the King and the Archbishop of
Canterbury. With their approval it was printed for
the use of the Scottish Church in 1637 ; and, although
it was never generally used, this "Scottish Prayer
Book" exercised considerable influence on the last
revision, by which the Prayer Book was brought
exactly to its present form in 1661.

During the great Rebellion the Puritans gained the
object which they had been pursuing for three generations. The Church was persecuted with
unrelenting hatred for fifteen years, and
during all that time the use of the Prayer
Book was made a crime. An "Ordinance" was passed
on Jan. 3, 1645, which forbade its use in any Church or
Chapel ; and one on the eve of St. Bartholomew, which

[marginal notes:]

A.D. 1604.
Hampton Court
Conference.

A.D. 1637.
The Scottish
Prayer Book.

Suppressed by
Puritans from
1645 to 1661.

forbade its use in private, and required all copies of it to be given up heavy penalties being imposed on those who dared to disobey these tyrannical injunctions. There were some brave and good men, however, who preferred to "obey God rather than man," and continued to celebrate Divine Service in spite of this heathenish persecution.

§ 5. *The existing Book of Common Prayer.*

THE Restoration of the Constitution of England brought about the Restoration of the Church of England as a necessary part of the Constitution.

Savoy Conference
A.D. 1661

Another attempt was now made to reconcile the Puritans to the Prayer Book, by means of an assembly similar to that held in the reign of James I. This met at the Savoy Palace in the Strand, and was hence called the "Savoy Conference." It was composed of twenty-one Divines on each side, its sittings lasting from April 15 to July 24, 1661. As usual, the Puritans showed themselves most provokingly ignorant and unreasonable. They intemperately required all the distinctive principles of the Church to be sponged out of the Prayer Book, and would be content with no less sweeping concessions; and thus they thoroughly defeated this last official attempt to draw them into unity with the Church.

A.D. 1662
The present
Prayer Book
settled.

The Convocations of Canterbury and York appointed Committees, however, to review the Prayer Book as it had been used before the Rebellion. These Committees were also authorized by letters patent to act for the Crown; and being thus turned into a Royal Commission, met at Ely House, in Holborn, and completed their work by

Dec. 20, 1661. The great and learned Cosin, Bishop of Durham, had marked a number of changes that he thought expedient in a folio Prayer Book of 1619, which is still preserved at Durham, and of which there is also a copy (in Archbishop Sancroft's handwriting) in the Bodleian Library, Oxford. This book was put into the hands of the Commissioners (of whom Cosin was one), and most of the suggestions were adopted. The revised Book having passed through the two Houses of Convocation, was then submitted to the King in Council, and by him was sent to Parliament, with a recommendation that it should be adopted in the Act of Uniformity then under the consideration of Parliament. No alterations were made in the Book after it left the Convocation; but it was attached to, and made part of the Act of Uniformity, which was made and passed by the Houses of Lords and Commons, and which received the Royal Assent on May 19, 1662. Very great care was used that every step of the Book's progress should be strictly constitutional; and when it was finally authorized by law, exact folio copies of it were certified by having the Great Seal and copies of the Letters Patent attached to The Sealed them, one of which was sent to every Books. Cathedral, to the Law Courts at Westminster, and to the Tower of London. Several of these are still preserved as perfect as they were on the day they were issued, and they are the legal authority to be referred to for the exact words of the Book of Common Prayer.

Another attempt was made by the Puri- Attempted re-tan party to alter the Prayer Book to their vision of 1689. views in 1689. But although a Commission was appointed by William III., and an altered Book produced, the attempt utterly failed. No further alterations were made after 1662 until 1871, when the Tables of Daily and Proper Lessons were reconstructed.

Adopted and translated for other Churches.
During that time it has been adopted by the American Church, and in the British Colonies. It has also been translated into the following languages and dialects, forty-two in number :—

Latin	Russian	Amharic
Greek	Polish	Telugoo
Hebrew	Modern Greek	Chinese
Welsh	Persian	Hawaiian
Irish	Turkish	Kafir
Gaelic	Armenian	Bullom
Manx	Armeno-Turkish	Yoruban
French	Arabic	Malay
German	Bengali	Dyak
Spanish	Hindi	Singhalese
Portuguese	Burmese	Indo-Portuguese
Italian	Mahratta	Cree
Dutch	Tamil	Malagasy
Danish	Susu	Maori

One of the most interesting facts connected with these translations is, that the Hawaiian version was made (in 1863) by the native King, Kamehameha IV., who also annexed to it a Preface, which shows a thorough knowledge of the principles of the Prayer Book.

This history of the Book of Common Prayer will show (1) how carefully it was originally constructed out of the ancient Service Books of the Church of England, which had their origin in Apostolic times : (2) that all changes in it have been made by the representative body of the Church, and confirmed by the representative body of the nation : (3) that it has kept its ground in the face of greater opposition and danger than any which it has met with in recent times.

CHAPTER II

The Prayer Book System of Divine Worship

" We know what we worship."—JOHN iv. 22.

THE leading principle of the Prayer Book is, that the public devotions of the Church must The Services consist chiefly of words and acts by which chiefly consist God is adored. Every thing that is to be of Adoration, said or done looks towards this purpose : so that even when instruction is given, as in the reading of Holy Scripture, it is mingled with the adoration offered in the Canticles ; while the very sermon ends, and often begins, with an ascription of praise to the Blessed Trinity.

The great central act of adoration is the Sacrifice of the Holy Eucharist, which enables the united to the Church on earth to hold communion with Intercession of Christ by the the One Mediator between God and man, Holy Eucharist. and thus to connect all parts of her devotions with the one prevailing intercession which He is continually making before the Throne of God. All the services are, therefore, constructed with a view to the principle expressed by the words, " Through Jesus Christ our Lord ; " and whether those words are used or not, it is to be understood that Sacraments, Prayers, Psalms,

C

Hymns, Benedictions, Absolutions, Confessions, and all other parts of Divine Service are coloured by this principle.

Thus the one great purpose for which we build Churches and frequent them, is that we may offer ADORATION (or Divine Worship) to God through our Lord Jesus Christ.

This explains the very large space which is occupied in the Services by " Psalms and Hymns and Spiritual Songs." If we take, for an example, Morning Prayer on the first day of the month, we have the *Venite Exultemus* and five other Psalms, the *Te Deum* and the *Benedictus*, besides the short hymn called *Gloria Patri*, the Apostles' Creed, which is also a kind of hymn, the Versicles at the beginning and in the middle of the Service, and the Anthem, or else a metrical hymn, which may be taken from some other source than the Prayer Book. Supposing the whole of Morning Prayer to occupy three-quarters of an hour, these " Psalms and Hymns and Spiritual Songs," will occupy at least two of those quarters ; and thus two-thirds of the Service is direct adoration offered in words of praise.

And because Adoration is the chief work of Divine Worship, a large amount of CEREMONIAL is used, after the pattern which God Himself revealed to Moses on Mount Sinai ; to Isaiah and to Ezekiel in their visions ; and, above all, to St. John in the Book of the Revelation. If we went to Church chiefly for the sake of being taught by the reading of Holy Scripture and the preaching of sermons, we need use little ceremony : but the Prayer Book principle is, that we go there to worship God ; and the worship of God must necessarily be of a highly cere-

[marginal note:] Thus so much Praise in our Services :

[marginal note:] so many Ceremonies,

monial character, whether offered by Angels and redeemed saints in Heaven, or by ourselves on earth.
All the ceremonies set down in the Prayer Book ought,
therefore, to be devoutly used, and many more also
which have come down to us by tradition from preceding generations ; such as turning to the Altar at the
Creed, saying "Glory be to Thee, O Lord," before
the Gospel, using the sign of the cross, bowing at the
name of the Holy Trinity and of Jesus, and others of
a like character. Those which are officially used by
the Clergy are, of course, used with the same object,
and on the same principle—that of adoring, or worshipping, God.

The same principle, likewise, explains why there is
so much SINGING in Divine Worship. For singing is
the highest and most beautiful use that can be made
of the human voice ; so that, as an organ _{and so much}
for singing, David calls the tongue "the _{Singing}
best member that I have," and bids it to join with instruments of music in the praise of God by such words
as "Awake up, *my glory*, awake, lute and harp." No
one would think that the glorious hymns which have
been revealed to us as used by the heavenly host could
be used by them in any other manner than by singing,
whether the "Holy, Holy, Holy," heard _{The songs of}
by Isaiah and St John, or the "Glory to _{Heaven.}
God in the highest," heard by the shepherds at Bethlehem, or the "Worthy is the Lamb" of the whole
communion of saints. We can scarcely even think of
them ourselves without "setting" them to some kind
of melody in our thoughts : the expression, "*songs
of angels*," comes to us quite naturally whenever we
speak of them as *worshipping :* and the "new song,"
and the "Song of Moses and of the Lamb," spoken of

in the Revelation, quite justify such a tone of thought
and expression.

And if we come to historical facts, it will be found
that to *speak* the praises of God in Divine Worship in
any other manner than by singing them, is quite a
recent invention, and an entire innovation upon the
practice of God's Church from the time of Moses to
the rise of Puritan habits in the sixteenth century—

of the Temple : a period of 3000 years. As soon as the
Israelites were a free people, " Then sang
Moses and the children of Israel this song unto the
Lord, and spake, saying, I will sing unto the Lord, for
He hath triumphed gloriously . the horse and his rider
hath He thrown into the sea " A similar national song
of triumphant praise was sung by Deborah and Barak.
And, though the psalmody of the Tabernacle is not
directly spoken of until the time of David, it could not
have been to unpractised choirs that he gave the com-
mand that they should bring up the Ark from its
captivity " with instruments of music, psalteries, and
harps, and cymbals, sounding by lifting up the voice
with joy " From his time, at least, and probably long
before his time, " the Levites, which were the singers,
arrayed in white linen," stood between the congregation and the altar, and day by day sang appointed
Psalms to God with accompaniments of " cymbals,
psalteries, harps, and trumpets " This mode of service
of the Primitive was continued in the Church of Christ ;
Church :   so that the singing of hymns was the
feature of its worship which was most noticed by the
heathen ; antiphonal chanting and responsive versicles are known to have been used in the very
earliest ages of Christianity; some of our Sacred Music
is supposed to come down to us from the Primitive

Church; and from the Divine Worship of mediæval
times our own system is directly derived. The old
words "read," "say," and "sing," are re- the pattern for
tained from the ancient rubrics, meaning those of the
the same as they always did, the more or England.
less elaborate kinds of musical recitation; the Psalms
are "pointed as they are to be sung in Churches;"
Canticles, Anthems, and Hymns intermingle with the
Prayers and the Lessons from Holy Scripture; and
the voice of Prayer itself ascends to God on the wings
of musical intonation and responsive harmony.

The devotional system of the Prayer Book is, therefore, a singing system; and the Church of England is
what the Mediæval, the Primitive, and the Jewish
Churches were, "a Singing Church." Psalms, Hymns,
Prayers, Creeds, Litanies, and Responses are all offered
to the praise and glory of God, "with the voice of
melody," through Jesus Christ our Lord.

And this leads us on to another principle, which is
conspicuous in every page of the Prayer Book; namely,
that its system of Divine Worship is one The great share
in which the people are intended to take of the Laity in
a large share. Choirs, of many "lay our Services.
clerks," or their solitary representative, *the* "Parish
Clerk," are simply the leaders of the congregation at
large; and neither are, nor ever were, intended to make
their voices a *substitute* for the voices of the whole
body. There is a priesthood which belongs to every
Christian, as St. Peter tells us; and this "priesthood
of the Laity" gives them the privilege, and imposes
upon them the duty, of taking their part in Divine
Service, not only in thought, but in act and word.
The Prayer Book shows, in fact, that there is almost
as much for the lay part of the congregation to say

and sing as there is for the Clergy; and even when the Priest *collects* their suffrages into an offering made by his own voice alone, the continual " Amen " of the people ratifies his offering, and adopts it by an audible

Silence of the assent A congregation which listens to
Laity wrong the Service, but does not join in it, is, therefore, behaving in a very different manner from what it is intended to do ; and in one quite contrary to the spirit of the Prayer Book. There may be individual persons here and there who, from infirmity or some other cause, cannot join audibly in the chorus of Divine Worship ; but those who can do so and neglect to do so, are forfeiting a privilege and leaving a duty undone.

These general principles being made clear, a few

The regular words will suffice to explain what are the
Services ordain- particular services ordained by the Church
ed in Prayer
Book. of England for carrying them out in her continual practice.

Weekly Com- 1 The HOLY COMMUNION is intended
munion to be celebrated in every Church at least on all Sundays and other Holy Days . for which purpose special Collects, Epistles, and Gospels are appointed, with Proper Prefaces on certain great Festivals. This celebration of the highest rite of Christianity strikes the key-note of the following week, and connects the other Services with the Intercession of our Lord by drawing down His Sacramental Presence, and making it a ladder between earth and Heaven.

Daily Com- In Cathedrals and Collegiate Churches
munion. where there are many clergy, it is the intention of the Prayer Book that there should be a

daily celebration of the Holy Eucharist; the Sunday Collects, &c., being appointed for use on every day of the following week.

2. A DAILY SERVICE of Morning and _{Daily Mattins} Evening Prayer, or "Mattins" and _{and Evensong.} "Evensong," is intended to be offered up in every Church. This practice was adopted from the Temple Services, and has always been observed in times when the Church has been vigorous and active.

3. The LITANY is to be sung on Sun- _{Litany three} days, Wednesdays, and Fridays, and at _{times a week.} other times when it shall be commanded by the Ordinary; that is, by the Bishop or his official representative.

Such continual public acts of Divine _{Reasons for} Worship are expedient for various reasons. _{daily services.} (1). It is due to the honour of Almighty God that the Church in every place consecrated to His service should begin and end the day by rendering to Him a service of praise. (2). Each Church and Parish being a corporate centre and corporate whole, prayer for God's grace and His mercy should be offered morning and evening for the body which that Church, and such congregation as can assemble, represents. Thus the Divine Presence is drawn down to the Tabernacle, that it may thence sanctify the whole camp. (3). It is a great benefit to the Clergy to offer Divine Worship, Prayer, and Intercession in the presence of, and in company with, some of their flock : and the Laity should never allow their Clergy to find the House of God empty when they go there to perform Divine Service. (4). There are spiritual advantages in such constant services which are found out by experience ; and when discovered are dearly cherished. (5). The Daily Mattins and Evensong in Church are the true and real form of Family Worship, for which the latter is but a very imperfect substitute.

CHAPTER III

𝕸orning 𝕻rager

"My voice shalt Thou hear betimes, O Lord: early in the morning will I direct my prayer unto Thee, and will look up."—PSALM v. 3.

THE Morning Prayer, or Mattins, of the modern Church of England was originally Origin of our formed out of the three very ancient Latin Morning Prayer. Services which were used between Midnight and 6 A.M. in monasteries, and which were called Mattins, Lauds, and Prime[1]. In practice these were very commonly made into one Service; and, as they were all three

---

[1] The daily services of the Church before its reformation were nominally as follows :—

MORNING PRAYERS. { *Nocturns*, or *Mattins*, before daybreak.
{ *Lauds*, at daybreak.
{ *Prime*, about six o'clock, "the first hour."

MIDDAY PRAYERS. { *Tierce*, at nine o'clock, "the third hour."
{ *Sexts*, at noon, "the sixth hour."
{ *Nones*, at three o'clock, "the ninth hour."

EVENING PRAYERS. { *Vespers*, an early evening service.
{ *Compline*, a late evening service at bedtime.

As public services, these were scarcely known to any of the Laity, except those who were monks or nuns; but they were in the Primers for private use, and translated into English. See p. 3.

almost exactly alike in the beginning, this caused some unmeaning repetition; as, for instance, " O God, make speed to save us," in three places. When the services were properly remoulded into one, as in the Prayer Book, this repetition was avoided.

In all these three services, as now in Morning How the Psalms Prayer, Psalms formed the principal por-were used. tion. The 51st, 63rd, 148th, 149th, 150th, and 119th (verses 1—32)[2] were used every day : the others, up to the 109th, being divided among the seven days of the week Each of the services was thus longer than our present Morning Prayer; and when joined together, they would have been much too long for the use of the Laity in public worship The present division of the Psalms was therefore substituted in 1549 ; and thus about one-fourth of the number appointed by the ancient rule adopted for the modern.

In the first Book of Common Prayer (1549), Mattins Short form of began with the Lord's Prayer, and ended Morning and with the third Collect ; and there are Evening Prayer reasons for thinking that this is still the form in which the Service is intended or permitted to be used in ordinary Churches on week days All before the Lord's Prayer was prefixed in 1552, and the intercessory prayers which follow the Anthem were added in 1661.

The original intention was, therefore, to open Morning Prayer with the words in which our Lord taught us to pray, as the Communion Service opens. But, in condensing the three ancient services, the reforming Divines of 1544-9 had unaccountably omitted the Con-

---

[2] The rest of Ps. cxix. was said every day at Tierce, Sexts, and Nones.

fession and Absolution, which had always been used towards the close of "Prime." To remedy this defect, our present Confession and Absolution were composed and placed at the beginning of the Service, and thus Uncatholic omission of 1549 remedied in 1552. the character of its opening was much changed. As it now stands, Morning Prayer may be divided into· five portions : (1). The Introduction, (2). The Praises, (3). The Lessons, (4). The Profession of Faith, (5). The Prayers.

§ 1. *The Introduction.*

THE SENTENCES are short "Invitatories" to Divine Service, very appropriately sung as anthems in some churches. Some of them are of a much more penitential character than others, marking the tone of the season of Lent. One is especially adapted for Advent ; and all may be so used as to distinguish particular days or seasons, thus "giving the key-note" to the Service which follows, and *inviting* all to worship in the spirit thus indicated.

THE EXHORTATION was prefixed to Morning Prayer at a time when daily public prayer was a novelty to the Laity, and when they were so ignorant of the true nature of Divine Worship that such a short homily on the subject had a practical use.

THE CONFESSION is to be said by all kneeling. The proper way of saying it is to repeat each clause (indicated by a capital letter) as soon as the Minister[3] has said the last word of that clause. It should always

---

[3] "Minister," in Prayer Book language, means "the person ministering," whether Bishop, Priest, Deacon, or (as in the Baptismal Service) Layman.

be said in monotone[4], that is, on one uniform musical
note, except in those churches (as Ely Cathedral)
where it is the custom to sing some of the clauses to
several notes, like a chant.

Being a " General Confession," it is framed in language which avoids the mention of particular sins ; and
•this language is substantially taken from Holy Scripture. The spirit in which it should be used is pointed
out in a rubric which precedes the Confession to be
used on board ship when there is danger of ship-
wreck .—

"When there shall be imminent danger, as many as can
be spared from necessary service in the Ship shall be called
together, and make an humble Confession of their sin to
God. In which every one ought seriously to reflect upon
those particular sins of which his conscience shall accuse
him."

THE ABSOLUTION is to be said only by a Priest (or
by a Bishop, since his office includes that of a priest
also), and is to be said by him *standing*, as a ceremonial sign that he is speaking with authority in the
name of God The absolving words are, " He par-
doneth and absolveth all them that truly repent, and
unfeignedly believe His holy Gospel ;" the meaning
of the latter words being, " those who unfeignedly believe His Gospel promise respecting Absolution."

As it is impossible for each person in a congregation
to confess his particular sins, it is impossible for the
priest to give more than a *general* absolution, which
looks neither to particular sins nor particular persons.
It is sown broadcast by the merciful Sower in whose

[4] "Monotone" is formed from two Greek words, *monos*,
one, *tonos*, sound.

name it is spoken. Some falls, in every large and mixed congregation, on stony ground, some by the way side, some among thorns ; but it is God's Word of Absolution, and where there is good ground, there it falls with absolving power, bringing that which its rubrical title indicates, " Remission of Sins."

THE LORD'S PRAYER is to be said "with" the Minister, word by word, not "after" him, as the Confession is said. It also should be said in "monotone," except where it is the practice to sing it as in chanting.

This Divine prayer should often be used with a "special intention," in which its various petitions are directed in a particular manner towards particular objects, as for example, " *Thy Kingdom come*, in the conversion of the heathen, in the Second Advent, in our hearts. *Thy will be done*, in the Church, in the State, in the case in which I am in doubt, in resignation to my affliction."

In this part of Divine Service it confirms and seals the Word of Absolution, and opens the door of Praise. But a Christian, who has learned how to apply the Lord's Prayer in the manner indicated above, will often find other uses for it here and elsewhere in public worship, so that a momentary thought may give it a new and present application and power.

§ 2. *The Praises.*

THE great central work of the Daily Offices is that of singing praise to God ; and chiefly in the words of that sweet singer, who belongs equally to God's ancient Israel and to His Christian Israel. To prepare ourselves for this work, we first sing " O Lord, open Thou our lips, and our mouth shall show forth Thy praise ;"

and then the hymn to the Blessed Trinity, "Glory be to the Father . . . . ." as a key to the meaning in which all such praises are sung.

THE VERSICLES, or little verses, are known with certainty to have been in use since the sixth century, and are probably part of the Apostolic Ritual. They are taken from Ps. li. 15, "O Lord, open Thou my lips ; and my mouth shall show forth Thy praise," and from Ps. lxx. 1, "Make haste, O God, to deliver me ; make haste to help me, O Lord :" the "me" being changed into "us" in 1552, to give a more congregational tone to them. They form a most fitting prefix to what follows, since, except God open our lips, we cannot show forth His praise to His glory. It should be remembered that these and all such versicles are used in the name of the Church, and that the *individual* application of them is subordinate to this chief application of them in the name of the one mystical body. Even the original "my" and "me" had the latter meaning ; as it often has in Scripture.

THE GLORIA PATRI comes down to us from the Primitive Church, and is naturally traceable to the angelic hymns in Isaiah vi. 3 and Luke ii. 14, the Trinitarian form of it being equally traceable to our Lord's words in Matthew xxviii. 19. It has been used in this part of Divine Service for at least 1300 years, and can be traced in such use for nearly as long a time in the Church of England. It also occurs in the same position in the daily offices of the Eastern and the Continental Churches ; so that, throughout the world, the Church Catholic opens its lips day by day with the same words of faith in the Blessed Trinity, praising and worshipping the Three in One and One in Three.

It is a very ancient and a very proper ceremony, to incline the head at the first half of this hymn as a humble gesture which recognizes the glory of God in three Persons ; and which follows the example set by the holy Angels when they veil their faces with their wings as they sing to the glory of the Trinity in the vision of Isaiah.

THE ALLELUIA, that is, " Praise ye the Lord," reminds us that we are joining in Divine Worship with the Church in heaven, which sings ever " Praise our God, all ye His servants, both small and great. . . . . Alleluia, for the Lord God omnipotent reigneth." (Rev. xix. 5, 6.)

THE VENITE, so called from the Latin words *Venite exultemus* with which the 95th Psalm opens, has been used as an " invitatory," or invitation to praise God in the Psalms, from the earliest days of Christianity, and was probably adopted from the Temple Service. In the ancient Church, it used to be interpolated with verses which adapted it to the various Christian seasons ; and these being dropped in 1549, the sentences at the beginning of Morning Prayer were introduced as a substitute for them (though rather a meagre one) in 1552.

On Easter Day, certain verses from St. Paul's Epistles to the Romans and the Corinthians are used instead of the *Venite*, which are printed before the Collect for Easter Day. These verses are sung to the praise of Christ in respect to His Resurrection : and it is to the praise of Christ that the Venite is to be sung, showing forth the glory of Him who is our Saviour and our King, by Whom all things were made, Who is the Good Shepherd and Bishop of our souls.

THE PSALMS are to be *said* (in monotone) by the

Minister and the congregation alternately, or *sung* (to chants) by the choir and congregation, verse by verse alternately, from the opposite sides of the Church[5].

The difference between the Prayer Book and the Bible English of the Psalms is explained by a notice at the beginning of the Prayer Book ·—" NOTE. That the Psalter followeth the Division of the Hebrews, and the Translation of the great English Bible, set forth and used in the time of King Henry the Eighth, and Edward the Sixth." The last revision of the Prayer Book was made more than half a century later than the last translation of the Bible, but it was considered that the older version of the Psalms was better adapted for singing, and not less true to the original words of the inspired writers. In the ancient Church of England, when daily services were sung only in Cathedrals and monastic Churches, the Psalter was sung through (according to a particular system) every week. But when the Book of Common Prayer was set forth, with a daily Service in which the Laity were intended to join, the present division was adopted, by which all the Psalms are sung through in the course of four weeks instead of seven days.

Meaning of the Psalms in Divine Service. The Psalter is to be used in Divine Service chiefly with reference to what is called its " Christology ;" that is, its application to our Lord and His Mystical Body the Church The Jewish sense of the Psalms has passed away; and they are now to be used in this Christian sense, of which every one of them is capable, and which is illustrated by the appropriation of some as " Proper

[5] This is called *antiphonal* singing, from two Greek words, meaning, *voice against voice.*

Psalms" on particular Holy Days. A careful study of these, of which the list is subjoined, will give a key to the proper use of the Psalms day by day in a Christian sense.

	MATTINS.	EVENSONG.
Christmas Day. .	Psalm 19	Psalm 89
. . . . . .	—— 45	—— 110
. . . . . .	—— 85	—— 132
Ash Wednesday .	Psalm 6	Psalm 102
. . . . . .	—— 32	—— 130
. . . . . .	—— 38	—— 143
Good Friday . .	Psalm 22	Psalm 69
. . . . . .	—— 40	—— 88
. . . . . .	—— 54	
Easter Day . .	Psalm 2	Psalm 113
. . . . . .	—— 57	—— 114
. . . . . . '	—— 111	—— 118
Ascension Day .	Psalm 8	Psalm 24
. . . . . .	—— 15	—— 47
. . . . . .	—— 21	—— 108
Whit Sunday . .	Psalm 48	Psalm 104
. . . . . .	—— 68	—— 145

This intelligent use of the Psalter will also be promoted by an investigation of the manner in which our Lord and His Apostles applied it in a mystical sense on many occasions, a few of which may be found by the following references: Luke xxiv. 44. Matt. xxi. 16, 42 ; xxii. 45. Luke xxiii. 46. John xiii. 18 ; xv. 25. Acts ii. 25, 31, 36. Rom. xv. 9, 11.

Using the Psalms in this way, it will soon be understood and felt that many solemn words and expressions which we should shrink from using with reference to ourselves, may be sung without hesitation when they are recognized as the words of Christ and His Church.

D

The sufferings, the condemnation of sinners, the triumphs, the exalted joys, spoken of in the Psalms, are Christ's or those of His mystical Body ; and they are spoken by us, not as expressions of personal feeling, but that by the singing of these inspired words, given to us by God for the purpose, we may make "the outgoings of the morning and evening to praise Him" day by day. It may also be remembered that the Gloria Patri sung after each Psalm seals this Christian sense of them, and connects them with that fuller knowledge of God which has been revealed in the coming and work of our Lord Jesus Christ.

§ 3. *The Lessons.*

AT Morning Prayer the two Lessons are taken from the books of the Old Testament, the Apocrypha, and the New Testament. The system on which they are read is as follows :

1. The Old Testament is read through, in selected portions, at the ordinary daily services ; some few passages in several books being omitted, as unsuitable for public reading. The four books of Kings and Chronicles are read together in such a manner as best to illustrate Jewish history, and the prophecy of Isaiah is put off until the middle of November, that it may come in during the season of Advent, on account of its special teaching respecting our Lord.

2. After the Old Testament has been read through (except Isaiah), the more edifying books of the Apocrypha are read for three weeks, from October 27th to November 18th.

3. The books of the New Testament are read over, chapter by chapter, at Morning Prayer on week-days

and Sundays : the only interruptions being a, few Proper Lessons on certain Holy Days.

4. Proper Lessons from the Old Testament, the Apocrypha, and the New Testament are appointed for Sundays and other Holy Days. These are selected with the view of illustrating (1) the general dealings of God with His ancient people, and (2) the particular circumstances which the Holy Days commemorate.

The object of reading Holy Scripture Lessons as acts in Divine Service is not only to instruct of Worship. the congregation, but also to set forth the glory of God. The Lessons are therefore to be regarded as acts of worship telling forth His marvellous works, His justice, and His love. And this is why they are followed by the CANTICLES, that the narration of God's dealings with His people may run up into acts of praise, by means of which even His written Word becomes an offering of adoration made in the Presence of His Divine Majesty.

In the ancient Church of England, from three to nine short Lessons were said at Mattins, and a Canticle or an Anthem was sung after each of them ; but in the Prayer Book two principal Canticles have been appointed for ordinary use, and two others which may be substituted under particular circumstances : all four having been taken from some part of the ancient Morning Services.

The TE DEUM has been sung at Mattins in the Church of England from time immemorial, probably for more than a thousand years. In its present form this glorious hymn comes down to us from the fourth century ; but a portion of it is quoted by St. Cyprian (A.D. 252), so that it represents a still more ancient hymn, and is thus traceable almost to Apostolic times.

It was anciently called the Hymn of St. Ambrose, or of St. Ambroşe and St. Augustine ; but probably the former only composed music for it—that known as the Ambrosian chant. An ancient tradition also associates it with the baptism of St. Augustine by St. Ambrose, asserting that they sang it in alternate verses on that occasion ; but there is good reason to think it was a well-known hymn of the Church long before they thus used it.

Explanation of the *Te Deum*   The. first ten verses of the *Te Deum* are an offering of praise to the Father Almighty, with the Scriptural recognition of the Blessed Trinity implied in the words which Isaiah heard the Seraphim sing when he beheld the glory of Christ, and spake of Him. In the three following verses this angelic song is developed into an ascription of praise to each Person,—the Father, infinite in Majesty, the Son the only begotten, and the Holy Ghost the Comforter. Praising the Unity and Trinity of the Divine Nature, the whole Church joins together with the voices of Angels, Cherubim, Seraphim, Apostles, Prophets, Martyrs, and the holy Church throughout the world ; adoring God in the Church Triumphant and in the Church Militant, and acknowledging Him as the Divine Object of all Divine Worship. Then begins (at the 14th verse) that part of the hymn in which God is praised for the work of the Incarnation, from " Thou art the King of Glory, O Christ," being all addressed to our Blessed Lord. In the last verses, with a mixture of triumph and plaintiveness, the Lord's first Advent is treated as leading on to His Second, for which our daily life is a preparation ; and the " let *me* never be confounded," reminds us of the individual interest which each has in the ·

work of Christ, and in the offering of praise and supplication by the body of the Church.

Thus the structure of the *Te Deum* fits it for linking together the Lessons from the Old Testament and from the Gospels; the vision of God in prophecy associating it with the one, and that of God Incarnate with the other.

The BENEDICITE is the hymn that was sung by the three Jewish young men when they were walking in the furnace with One like unto the Son of God. It was used in Divine Service as early as the time of St. Chrysostom, and was sung every Sunday, with the Psalms, in the ancient Church of England. When this and the other Old Testament hymns (the songs of Isaiah, Hezekiah, Hannah, Habakkuk, and Moses) were struck out of the Psalter in 1549, this was placed here to be used in Lent instead of the *Te Deum*. But it is scarcely appropriate to that season, being of so joyous a character; and, as the rubric now stands, it may be used at any fitting time in the place of the former Canticle.

The BENEDICTUS was a Sunday Canticle in the ancient Church of England, and appears to have been used in the same way from the time of the great St. Benedict in the sixth century. It is here used as a thanksgiving to Almighty God for His mercy shown to mankind in the Incarnation of our Lord, as told by the Gospel Lessons, and in the foundation of His Church, as told in the Acts. It is the last prophecy of the Old Dispensation and the first of the New, giving the key to an Evangelical interpretation of all prophecies under the one, by which they are connected with the other, and declaring the unity of the faithful under both in the One Lord.

The JUBILATE was also a Sunday Canticle in the ancient Church of England, and was placed here in 1552 to be used on Feb 18th, June 17th, June 24th, and Oct. 15th, when the *Benedictus* is read in the Second Lesson itself.

§ 4. *The Profession of Faith.*

THE recitation of a Creed in Divine Service is of very ancient origin, and has formed part of the daily Offices of the Church of England as long as they can be traced back, that is, to 300 years before the time of the Norman Conquest. The Athanasian Creed was used daily, as well as that of the Apostles, until 1549 ; but since that time it has been appointed to be used instead of it on thirteen festivals ; the intention being that it should be said once a month, and on Trinity Sunday.

THE APOSTLES' CREED can be traced in its present form as far back as the ninth century in English, and as the year 390 in Latin. The substance of it is also found, in Greek, as early as the year 190, and in such a form as to lead to the belief that the writer who gives it—Irenæus—was simply putting into his own words what was commonly recited in some part of Divine Service. Whether or not it was actually composed by the Apostles, is uncertain ; but the statement that it was so is 1500 years old at the least ; and some strong evidence in its favour is given by St. Paul's references to a Form of sound words in passages like Rom. vi. 17 ; xvi. 17. Heb. x. 23. Phil. iii. 16. 2 Tim i. 13. There is, in fact, more reason for believing that it was composed by the Apostles under the inspiration of the

Holy Ghost, at their last meeting, than for believing
the contrary.

THE ATHANASIAN CREED is also found in English
as early as the ninth century, and in Latin as early as
the year 570. It was composed in the first half of the
fifth century, either by Victricius, Bishop of Rouen
(A.D. 401), or by St. Hilary, Bishop of Arles, who died
A.D. 449. It has been called the Creed of St. Athana-
sius since the Council of Autun (A.D. 670), but most
likely only because its statements are such as were
made by that great theologian in maintaining the
belief of the Church against the heretic Arius. The
substance, and in many cases the very words of it,
may be found in still earlier writers. Its language
and statements have been very much objected to by
those who could not understand it, or who sympa-
thized with Anti-Christian heresies; but it is an in-
valuable treasury of sound doctrine respecting the
Holy Trinity and the Incarnation; and the more a
person believes in God and in our Lord Jesus Christ,
the more will he believe the Athanasian Creed.

The central position of the Profession of Faith in
Mattins and Evensong gives it a twofold meaning and
aspect. First, the Creed sums up the Scriptures which
have been said in the two Lessons, to the praise of
God and for the edification of the Church; and,
Secondly, it forms an introduction to the Prayers, the
language of true prayer being always founded on that
of true belief.

§ 5. *The Prayers.*

THE concluding section of Morning Prayer consists
of Prayers; the Lord's Prayer, the Suffrages, the Col-

lects, and the Intercessions. These are preceded by the ancient mutual Benediction of the Priest and people, " The Lord be with you. And with thy spirit." The substance of this benediction is found in Ruth ii. 4, Psalm cxxix. 8, and 2 Thess. iii. 16; and it is believed to have been handed down from the Apostles in its present form. It should be said while Priest and people are still standing.

THE LORD'S PRAYER is here introduced by the *Lesser Litany*, each of the three versicles of which was anciently said three times. This prefix is only omitted at the Holy Communion, in the Baptismal and Confirmation Offices, and at the beginning of Morning and Evening Prayer. In the latter case the Confession is used instead, and in the former it is omitted because the Lord's Prayer is there used as a Thanksgiving. As a rule, it should always be used before the Lord's Prayer, this being a primitive custom, and also appealing to the instinct of Christian humility, which shrinks from speaking to God in the words of our Lord without first asking His mercy even for our act of prayer, imperfect as it must be to His all-searching Eye. Our Lord's Prayer is used in this part of the Service as the introduction to other prayers, as it was previously used to introduce the Praises of the Service.

THE SUFFRAGES are all taken from the ancient Morning Service of the Church of England; but their original source is Holy Scripture, as follows :—

"Shew us Thy mercy; O Lord: And grant us Thy salvation."	} Ps. lxxxv. 7.
"O Lord, save the King: And hear us in the day we call upon Thee."	} Ps. xx. 9. Septuagint version.

"Let Thy priests be clothed with
 righteousness:
And let Thy saints shout for joy."
} Ps. cxxxii. 9.

"Save Thy people:
And bless Thine inheritance."
} Ps. xxviii. 9.

["Give peace in our time," &c., was substituted in 1549 for Ps. cxxii. 7, "Peace be within Thy walls," &c., or, "Grant us peace in Thy strength," as in the older forms. The present words are those of an ancient response or antiphon, attached to the Collect for Peace.]

"Create in me a clean heart, O God:
And take not Thy Holy Spirit from
 me."
} Ps. li. 10, 11.

In these Suffrages the people exercise their office as "a chosen generation, a royal priesthood, an holy nation, a peculiar people, *that ye should show forth the praises* of Him Who hath called you out of darkness into His marvellous light." They are usually sung to a very beautiful form of musical recitation, which has been thus used for many ages in the Church of England.

THE COLLECTS at Morning Prayer are those for the Day, for Peace, and for Grace. Both the latter are exact translations from the ancient Latin ; and of the eighty-three Collects for the Day, only twenty-two were originally composed in English.

THE COLLECT FOR THE DAY connects the Daily Office with the Holy Eucharist, from the celebration of which it is borrowed ; and thus it is a link between all the praises and prayers of Mattins and the great Sacrifice on whose wings they are carried up to Heaven. Its weekly or festival variation is also a constant memorial before God of the times and seasons which He Himself has ordained, both in the natural and the spiritual world.

THE COLLECT FOR PEACE has been used at our Morning Service for 1,250 years. It is a prayer, first, for the peace of the Church Militant, bound to that service which is perfect freedom, and at war with spiritual foes against whose assaults God only can defend it ; and, secondly, for the peace of each Christian Soldier in the army of Christ, that his own part of the work and warfare may be ordered to a peaceful and joyful end.

THE COLLECT FOR GRACE is of equal antiquity with the preceding. It was originally intended to end the Morning Service, sending each worshipper forth from the Church to his daily occupation fresh from a prayer in which he had asked God to give him His grace that he might do his duty faithfully in that state of life to which he is called. But the intercessory prayers were subsequently inserted in the Prayer Book to be used in this place ; and then THE ANTHEM was interposed as the commencement of what is in fact a separate service, expanded from the ancient " Bidding of the Bedes." Where no Anthem is used, the Mattins should still end with the Collect for Grace.

THE INTERCESSIONS represent ancient prayers, but are most of them modern compositions.

THE PRAYER FOR THE QUEEN is found in its earliest form in a book of Prayers compiled for the use of Catharine Parr, the wife of Henry VIII., but inserted as it now stands in 1661. That FOR THE ROYAL FAMILY was placed at the end of the Litany in James the First's reign, in the year 1604, and in Mattins in 1661.

THE PRAYER FOR THE CLERGY AND PEOPLE is very ancient indeed, traceable in English for nearly 500, and in Latin for 1,400, years.

THE PRAYER OF ST. CHRYSOSTOM is translated from the Greek original in the Liturgies of St. Basil and St. Chrysostom, and it is not found in any other Services than those of the Eastern Churches and the Church of England.

THE BENEDICTION, or "Grace," is supposed to have been taken by St. Paul from the Liturgy used in Apostolic times. It was anciently used in the service of Tierce (the nine o'clock prayers) and was thence transferred to the end of Mattins in 1661.

Of the OCCASIONAL PRAYERS nothing more need be said than that they are part of the Intercessions, to be used before the Prayer of St. Chrysostom when occasion requires.

CHAPTER IV

The Litany

"Let the priests, the ministers of the Lord, weep between the porch and the altar, and let them say, Spare Thy people, O Lord."—JOEL ii. 17.

LITANIES were originally constructed to be sung in procession, and hence were commonly called "Processions" in England during the mediæval period. There is no doubt, however, that the whole of the Litany, as it is now used, was often sung at a faldstool in front of the Altar, as at present, and that the Procession itself usually ended with the singing of the latter part of the Litany in the same manner ; and this practice is so extremely similar in character to that referred to by the prophet, that it is difficult not to suppose it had its origin in the Temple Service.

Processional use of Litany.

But the common account of Litanies is, that they were invented by Mamertus, Bishop of Vienne, during a terrible succession of earthquakes which devastated that city about the year 467. This supposed first use of the Litany procession was on the three days before Ascension Day; and the earliest name given to such processions was that of

Its origin.

Rogations, a name strikingly appropriate to the petitions of the Litany, but since retained only as the designation of the three days mentioned.

The use of Litanies was gradually extended to many other occasions than those of the Rogation Its general Days' processions, and they soon became, popularity.
as they have ever since been, the most popular of all services. They were used before the general Easter Eve Baptisms, at Ordinations, at the Dedication of Churches, at Coronations, and before almost all services of an exceptional or occasional kind, just as, at the present day, before Confirmations ; and, in case of any public calamity, the " Processions " were immediately enjoined with special reference to it.

The Litany now used in the Church of The English England is substantially derived from the Litany.
ancient Form thus used in processions from about the 8th century. It had been translated into English for some centuries before the Reformation, but was only set forth in English for public use in the year 1544. In mediæval times a great number of Invocations of Angels, Apostles, and Saints were added after the four Invocations of the Divine Persons and the Holy Trinity, but these were now removed : a few clauses were taken away, and some new ones added, and in 1549 the Litany was brought into the Book of Common Prayer as it now stands.

The first three clauses of the Litany are Explanation of prayers offered to each Person of the the Litany.
Blessed Trinity, and are called *The Invocations.* They are acts of adoration, ending with a general prayer for mercy; thus following the example of one whose cry to our Lord forms part of this beautiful Form of prayer, " Son of David, have mercy upon me." The fourth

clause is a similar act of adoration and prayer offered
to the whole Blessed Trinity, "three Persons, and one
God."

Then follows a long series of short prayers, which
Its Prayers   are all addressed to our Blessed Lord,
to Christ   beginning with "Remember not, Lord,
our offences," and ending at the Lord's Prayer. Those
which begin with the word "From" are called *"Deprecations,"* and relate to the sins or dangers of
national or individual life, from which we pray Christ,
as our Good Lord, that He will deliver us. The
clauses beginning with the word "By" are called *"Obsecrations,"* and plead the acts and sufferings of our
Redeemer as each having a delivering power. After
these is a short summary of all the preceding prayers,
containing a world of meaning in its few words, asking
Christ to deliver us by the virtue of His sufferings and
triumph, alike when we are in trouble or in prosperity,
during life, and "in the hour of death," and in that
which comes after death, "the day of judgment."

Those clauses beginning "That it may please Thee,"
are called *Petitions* or *Supplications,* and are prefaced
with the significant acknowledgment, "We *sinners* do
                    beseech Thee to hear us." They first
Its intercessory supplicate Christ, our "Lord God," and
character   our "good Lord," for the Church as a
whole ; then for the Sovereign and the Royal Family,
for the Clergy, and for the Sovereign's counsellors and
deputies in the government of the kingdom and in the
administration of justice. After these supplications,
follow others for God's Blessing upon all Christians in
general, for all nations in general, for the increase of
ourselves in love and obedience, for the advancement
of all Christians in grace, and for the conversion of

those who are not yet in the way of truth. Then follow touching supplications for persons in various troubles and dangers, for God's mercy to all men, and for our enemies : the whole closing with a prayer for His blessing on the works of our hands, and for His forgiveness of all our sins, negligences, and ignorances.

This short summary of the Invocations, Deprecations, Obsecrations, and Supplications of the Litany, will show how very comprehensive a Form of Prayer it is, and how large a field it opens for the Christian to carry out the Apostolic injunction, " I exhort therefore that . . . . supplications, prayers, intercessions . . . . be made for all men."

With the Lord's Prayer—preceded by the " Kyrie Eleison " or Lesser Litany—begins the second half of the Litany, in which the responsive form of prayer is still largely retained, but which, not being intended for processional use, but to be said before the altar, drops the regular beat of prayer and response which is so conspicuous in the former half. The whole of this is translated and condensed from the ancient Latin, except the Prayer of St. Chrysostom, which was first added in the English Litany of 1544.

The Litany chant. The beautiful music to which the Litany is usually sung, was adapted for English words from the ancient service under the immediate supervision of Archbishop Cranmer. He also arranged other " Processions " for public use ; but Henry VIII. would not allow their publication, and they have now been lost.

CHAPTER V

Œvening Prayer

"It shall come to pass, that at evening time it shall be light."
ZECH. xiv. 7.

AS the Morning Service of the modern Church of England was formed out of its three ancient Morning Services, so its Evensong was compiled from the two ancient Evening Services of *Vespers* and *Compline*. Until 1661 it began with the Lord's Prayer, and ended with the third Collect; but the Sentences, &c., which had been prefixed to Mattins in 1552, were then prefixed to Evensong also, and the Intercessory Prayers were at the same time added at the end of both.

Its origin.

In the ancient Services the thirty-eight Psalms— 110—147—were divided among the Vespers of the week, and the 4th, 31st (verses 1—7) 91st and 134th were used every evening at Compline. But the present mode of using the Psalms was adopted for Evening as well as for Morning Prayer in 1549. The *Venite* has never been used before the Psalms of the Evening, the Invitation which it offers to praise God extending throughout the day.

How the Psalms were anciently sung.

THE FIRST LESSONS at Evening Prayer are appointed in continuance of the system adopted at Morning Prayer; but the Canticles are different.

THE MAGNIFICAT was used in the Primitive Church at an early Morning Service, that of " Lauds ;" but, as early as A.D. 820, it had found a place in Vespers ; and the English Church has used it in her Evensong for at least 800 years. It fulfils the same office towards the Lessons that the *Te Deum* does at Morning Prayer, linking together the Old and the New Dispensations. But the *Magnificat* is more closely associated with our Blessed Lord than any other hymn of the Church, and so has been held in special honour out of love to Him. For it was spoken by the Blessed Virgin, under the inspiration of the Holy Ghost, during the very time when the Divine overshadowing was causing her to be the Mother of our Lord. She offered up her thanksgiving to God because He had remembered His mercy and His ancient covenant by making His Son incarnate through her ; and the Church offers up her thanksgiving to Him daily in the same words, because through her the mystical Body of Christ is being continually brought forth to the promotion of His glory. As the other Canticles are, so also is this sung to the praise of the Personal WORD as revealed in the written Word—to the praise of God in Christ, revealed in the Old Testament as well as in the New.

The Cantate Domino was not used in any other way than as a Saturday morning Psalm in the ancient Church of England ; but it was placed here in 1552 as an alternative Canticle, that might be used after the First Lesson. The only occasion on which it seems desirable to use it, is when Evensong is repeated ; in which case it might be used at the first Evening Ser-

E

vice, the *Magnificat* being always reserved for the latest.

THE SECOND LESSONS are taken from the New Testament, which is thus read over in the course of every year, in the evening as well as in the morning. The course of reading is, for the Acts of the Apostles to be begun on January 1st, the Gospels on July 6th, and the Revelation (taking up the chapters from Morning Prayer) in the last fortnight of the year.

First Lessons are appointed for two Evensongs by the revision of 1871, and where there is only one Evensong, either of these may be used. Where no Proper Second Lessons are appointed, the Minister may select for the Second Evensong any chapter from the Gospels, or any of the Lessons appointed from them, setting aside the Lesson of the day.

THE NUNC DIMITTIS is their proper Canticle, having been so used from the earliest ages of the Church. It is so fitted for Evensong as to seem written for the purpose. Like the words of David, " I will lay me down in peace and take my rest, for it is Thou, Lord, only that makest me to dwell in safety," it is the aspiration of that faith which can behold Christ lightening the darkness of all night, and fulfilling the words of the prophet, "It shall come to pass that at evening time it shall be light." As the Gospels of the Morning Lessons reveal to us the Day Spring from on high visiting us, so the Epistles of the Evening Lessons reveal the Light of Christ's glory enlightening the Gentile as well as the Jewish world. The tone of the Canticle is singularly in agreement with that of the whole Evening Service ; the tone of those whose work for the day is done, and who look solemnly, yet not gloomily, to that night when "no man can work," but in which "there remaineth a rest for the people of God," through the salvation which Christ has prepared.

THE DEUS MISEREATUR was the fourth Psalm in the Sunday Lauds of the ancient Church, but was placed here in 1552. The remarks made respecting the *Cantate Domino* apply to this Canticle also.

THE COLLECT FOR PEACE comes from the same ancient source as that used in Morning Prayer. Placed here with the intention of making it nearly the last word of Evensong, it forms a sweet cadence of prayer leading on to the last notes of the third Collect. It follows very exactly the tone of the *Nunc Dimittis*, ringing with a gentle echo of the peace which lies beyond this world, as well as of the peace which the world cannot give, nor the soul entirely receive while it is in the world. In the Morning Collect the prayer is that of one who is asking God of His great mercy to bless and co-operate with His own in their strife against spiritual foes ; but in the evening the words are more those of one who is no longer able to struggle with his enemies, but looks to his Lord God alone to be his defence and his shield.

THE COLLECT FOR AID AGAINST ALL PERILS is equally ancient with the preceding, and has been used at Evening Prayer from the days of the Primitive Church. Here again the tone of the Nunc Dimittis is followed up ; and no words could be found which could be more appropriate for ending that service in which the Church and the individual Christian is committed to the care of a loving Father during the hours of darkness.

The remaining portions of Evening Prayer are identical with the corresponding parts of Morning Prayer, and do not, therefore, call for further notice.

CHAPTER VI

The Holy Communion

" This do in remembrance of Me."—LUKE xxii. 19.

THE Service for the Celebration of the Holy Eucharist is derived from the ancient Missal of the Church of England, which was also derived from the ancient Liturgy of the Church of Ephesus, brought to France, Spain, and Britain soon after the death of St. John. It underwent little alteration in being translated for the first Book of Common Prayer, but was more changed in 1552. Some subsequent revision has all tended towards a restoration of the more ancient forms.

Origin of English Liturgy.

This Service may be best understood by considering it as composed of six sections,—The Introduction, the Offertory, the Preparation of the Communicants, the Sacrifice, the Communion, and the Thanksgiving.

Its structure.

§ 1. *The Introduction.*

This portion of the Liturgy[1] extends as far as the end of the Nicene Creed, including the Sermon. It

[1] The word "Liturgy" properly belongs only to the Service for the celebration of the Holy Eucharist.

has been a too common practice to use no other part of the Communion Service except on the first Sunday of the month, or even more rarely; but this is contrary to the spirit of the Prayer Book, which provides for the whole of the Service being used whenever the Introduction is said, especially on all Sundays and other Holy Days, for which Collects, &c., are appointed.

THE LORD'S PRAYER is said here, as every where else in Divine Service, with a special object, and not as a pointless repetition. The Celebrant (that is, the Priest or Bishop who is to consecrate the elements) uses it for himself (and therefore it is not repeated by the people) as a prevailing intercession connected with his particular duty, that he may be found not unworthy to represent his Lord the Chief Priest of the Church in the offering of the Holy Eucharist. It should be heard, and mentally joined in by the people, with the same special object, since the offering to be made is made by them in conjunction with their leader who stands at their head in front of God's Altar. The " Amen " is to be said only by the Priest, as the type in which it is printed is meant to show.

THE COLLECT FOR PURITY is a prayer of the early Church, and has been used in its present place in the Church of England for at least 800 years ; but it has no place in the Roman Liturgy. Like the Lord's Prayer preceding, it is a part of the Celebrant's preparation for his duty, and of the laity for theirs. Standing at the head of his flock, the Priest offers up this preliminary prayer to God for himself and for them, that all may have their hearts cleansed from evil and wandering thoughts, and prepared for the solemn rite in which they are about to take their respective parts.

THE TEN COMMANDMENTS were read in English, and expounded to the people with great frequency in the ancient Church of England ; and this habit probably led to their use in this introductory portion of the Communion Office. The *Kyrie Eleison*, or Lesser Litany, was also said *nine* times (as at the end of the Litany) after the Collect for Purity. The change made was, therefore, to substitute the one response now used nine times, instead of the two "*Lord* have mercy," " *Christ* have mercy," to add the tenth, and to say the Commandments in a Liturgical or ritual manner, instead of as the text of a Sermon.

The " KYRIE ELEISON" here used is a Christian application of the Decalogue, in the words of Jeremiah xxxi. 33, and Psalm cxix. 36, and as already made by St. Paul in Hebrews viii. 10. It may be traced in Psalm cxix. 34, 36, and 112.

The Commandments and the Response together form an Eucharistic Litany : such prayers for obedience to God's law following the tone of the preceding Collect for purity of heart.

THE COLLECT FOR THE SOVEREIGN is given in two forms, both of which are believed to be derived from ancient Latin prayers, of which many similar to these two are extant. Its insertion in this part of the Communion Service, in addition to the intercession for the Sovereign in the " Prayer for the Church Militant," arose partly from temporary reasons connected with the great disloyalty of many persons at the time of the Reformation. But in the ancient Eucharistic Litany of the Eastern Church there is a similar prayer " For our most religious and God-protected Sovereigns, for all their Court and their Army, let us beseech the Lord. Lord have mercy upon us."

THE COLLECT OF THE DAY is one of eighty-three which are prefixed to their respective Epistles and Gospels, and which are framed with especial reference to those Scriptures, as the latter are selected with reference (in general) to some person or event commemorated before God at that particular season.

Of these Collects the greater number are known to have been in use in the Church of England for at least 800 years, that is, since St. Osmund revised our services in 1085. But they have probably been used by our Church much longer, as they are of much older date. Five of them are extant in the Sacramentary of St. Leo, A.D. 451 ; twenty-one in that of Gelasius, A.D. 492 ; twenty-eight in that of St. Gregory, A.D. 590 ; and seven are translations of other equally ancient prayers or Anthems. The remaining twenty-two were composed for the Book of Common Prayer, many expressions being, however, borrowed from ancient sources.

This concise and beautiful form of prayer was originally called the "Collect," because it is a gathering together of the supplications of many into one by the voice of the Priest, while in prayers and versicles he and the people pray alternately. But we need not confine the meaning to this, for it is equally true of the Eucharistic Collects, that they gather together in one short prayer the leading ideas of the Epistle and Gospel ; and the Collect in the Litany condenses into a focus all the preceding supplications. It is a form of prayer founded on the model given to us by our Lord, and the only two Prayers of the Church in the New Testament (Acts i. 24, 25, and Acts iv. 24—30) are of this character. The *petition* itself is always very simple, is generally introduced by some *reason*

why that special petition is offered, and is followed by
an act of adoration, in which the Mediatorial office of
our Lord is usually named Such careful and me-
thodical construction makes the Collects of the Communion Service more condensed and forcible in their
language than any other forms of prayer ; and they
dwell on the memory like effective strains of song.

THE EPISTLE AND GOSPEL represent the oldest
form in which Holy Scripture was read in the Christian
Church. The Holy Eucharist was, indeed, celebrated
for nearly twenty years before St Paul wrote his first
Epistle, and for nearly thirty years before the first
Gospel was written by St. Matthew. But there can be
little doubt that portions of the Old Testament were
even then read ; and that the New Testament Scriptures were used in the same way as soon as they were
completed and generally circulated. Our present
arrangement of the Epistles and Gospels is (with a
very few exceptions) that of the ancient English
Missal[2]; and was originally derived from a " Lection-
ary," arranged by St. Jerome about A.D. 370.

The principle of their selection is that of illustrating
the two great divisions of the Christian
year, from Advent to Trinity, and from
Trinity to Advent. In the first, our
Blessed Lord is set before us in a life-like diorama of
Gospels, which tell us about Him and His work, not
as in a past history, but as if the events were now
passing before us ; so that the Gospels are, as regards
Holy Scripture, what the *Obsecrations* of the Litany
are as regards Prayer, a memorializing before God of

Arrangement of Epistles and Gospels

---

[2] This differs in many cases from the arrangement of the
Roman Missal, and, where it differs, agrees with St. Jerome.

the Acts of Christ. In the second half of the year, the long-drawn season of Trinity, we see illustrated the Faith and Practice of the Church : her continuance, by the power of the Pentecostal outpouring, in the true faith of the Blessed Trinity, her practical following of her Master and Head through a long probationary career.

It must be observed that the Epistles are arranged on a principle of consecutive reading similar to that of the daily Lessons, but that there are many striking harmonies between them and the Gospels.

The reading of the Gospel has always *Ceremonies at* been treated with special reverence in the *reading the* Communion Service. All stand to hear *Gospel.* it, and, before it is read, sing the versicle, " Glory be to Thee, O Lord :" both practices being handed down from the ancient Church. In many Churches it is also the custom to sing " Thanks be to Thee, O Lord " at the end of the Gospel. Such short hymns are similar in their application to the Canticles of Morning and Evening Prayer.

THE NICENE CREED follows the reading of the Gospel as the Apostles' or Athanasian Creed follows the Second Lesson. It is an expanded form of the Apostles' Creed, adopted by more than 300 Bishops at the Council of Nicæa in the year 325. This Council set it forth only as far as "I believe in the Holy Ghost." The remaining clauses being added by the Council of Constantinople, A.D. 381. It is the most authoritative Profession of Faith possessed by the Christian Church, and is therefore placed here in its most solemn service. When a SERMON is preached at the time of the celebration of the Holy Communion, it is to be preached immediately after the Creed : for as the Creed declares the Faith contained in Holy Scripture, so ought the Sermon to be grounded on and regulated by the doctrine stated in the Creed.

§ 2. *The Offertory.*

AFTER the Sermon the Celebrant again takes his place before the Table of the Lord, for the purpose of making a solemn offering of the Bread and Wine which are afterwards to be consecrated. If there are any alms for the poor, or other devout offerings of the people (such as money or goods for the service of God), they are also offered at the same time, that such gifts to Him from Whom all things come may be sanctified by the Altar on which they are placed, and by His Presence there.

Until the time of the Offertory it is customary (the custom being significant but not essential) to keep the Bread and Wine standing on a *Credence-table* at the side of the Chancel, and not upon the Lord's Table. This custom (or any other by which the " Elements " are brought to the Altar at the moment when they are to be offered) makes the " Oblation of the Elements " a plain and important ceremony, as it has always been from the time of the Primitive Church. The Bread is first placed upon the Altar, then a little Water is added to the Wine (in accordance with a practice as old as the Church itself), to signify the union of the Divine and Human Natures in Christ, and as a lively memorial of Him Who "did shed out of His most precious side both water and blood ," and this " mixed Cup " is also placed on the Altar.

THE PRAYER FOR THE CHURCH is then said by the Celebrant, this being in reality the beginning of the

Consecration, although the "Preparation of the Communicants" comes in afterwards between it and the Act of Consecration.

The object of this Prayer is (1) to commend to God the gifts which are then lying upon His Table, both "alms" and "oblations;" and also (2) to commend to Him the whole body of the Church, living and departed[3], at a time when the offering up of the Eucharist makes intercession a special duty of love, and gives to it a special hope of prevailing power. Such intercessions at such a time have been used by the Church of Christ from the earliest ages to which we can trace Christian customs; and they are one chief means towards drawing closer that Communion of Saints in which we so often profess our belief.

§ 3. *The Preparation of the Communicants.*

THE CONFESSION[4] follows, after an Invitation to "draw near with faith," in which the principal words come from the primitive Liturgy of St. James. It is a "general" Confession, similar in character to that used at Morning and Evening-Prayer, not mentioning particular sins, but which each person who uses it may

[3] The Mediæval heading of this prayer containing the phrase "Church militant here on earth," has been supposed to exclude the departed; but the very prayer from which the heading (or "Oremus") is taken, mentions "all the faithful, living *and departed*," just as the present prayer does.

[4] The Exhortations and Invitation to draw near do not require any special notice. The former are very instructive Homilies; but the more they have been read, the less people have seemed to believe the statements which they contain. The Exhortation at the time of Communion is grounded on a Mediæval form, which is printed in the "Annotated Book of Common Prayer," page 179.

use as the expression of penitence for sins that have
been thought of one by one beforehand with penitent
sorrow. Its Mediæval original (in English) stood *after*
the Consecration, but of course before Communion :
and the change of place is made that the whole Congregation, as well as the Celebrant and his Ministers,
may humbly ask God's pardon before approaching the
last solemn Act which brings down Christ's Sacramental Presence.

THE ABSOLUTION is also general in its form, the
latter half being translated from the ancient Latin. It
conveys what it professes to convey—pardon and deli-
verance from sin to those whose Confession has been
honest and true ; and the pardon so conveyed is confirmed and sealed by the Sacred Communion afterwards effected between the Absolver Christ, and those
who have been absolved. It is to quicken the faith of
the latter in such an absolving Presence of Christ, that
the COMFORTABLE WORDS are introduced after the
Absolution. They are not found in any other Liturgy,
but are dear to the English ear.

§ 4. *The Sacrifice.*

THE first object for which the Holy Eucharist is celebrated is, that a memorial of Christ's Sacrifice may be
made by means of it. This memorial is made to GOD :
our Lord's words, "This do in remembrance of Me,"
meaning " This offer for ' a memorial' of Me ' before
the Lord your God [5].'" The Holy Eucharist is therefore *consecrated* before it is partaken of ; and the Con-

---

[5] See Numb. x. 10. The word here translated "do" is
translated "offer" in more than fifty places in the Holy
Bible ; and thus means "do sacrifice," as in Jer xxxiii. 18

secration is a memorial offering, or Sacrifice, of that
which the Bread and Wine become by consecration—
the Body and Blood of our Lord Jesus Christ.

This solemn Act of Consecration is preceded by an Act
of Praise and Worship, and by a " Prayer of Humble
Access" which marks the approach of the most sacred
portion of all Divine Service. The Act of Praise and
Worship consists of four Versicles, the Preface, and the
Sanctus. All these are found almost word for word in
every known Liturgy, in every part of the Catholic
Church, from the earliest times ; and there can be no
doubt that they come down from the Apostolic age.
No better commentary has ever been written on this
part of Divine Service than that which was made
by St. Cyril, Bishop of Jerusalem (A.D. 348), and delivered in one of his Catechetical Homilies, near to the
very spot where the Holy Eucharist was instituted.
" After this," he says, " the Priest cries aloud ' *Lift up
your hearts.*' For truly ought we in that most awful
hour to have our heart on high with God, and not be-
low, thinking of earth and earthly things. The Priest
then, in effect, bids all in that hour abandon all worldly
thoughts or household cares, and to have their heart
in heaven with the merciful God. Then ye answer,
' *We lift them up unto the Lord ;*' assenting to him
by your avowal . . . Then the Priest says, ' *Let us give
thanks to the Lord.*' For in good sooth are we bound
to give thanks, that He has called us, unworthy as we
are, to so great grace ; that He has reconciled us
who were His foes ; that He has vouchsafed to us the
spirit of adoption. Then ye say, ' *It is meet and
right.*' for in giving thanks we do a meet thing and a
right ; but He did, not a right thing, but what was
more than right, when He did us good, and counted us

meet for such great benefits." In the same Homily, St. Cyril also speaks of the SANCTUS, or TER SANCTUS[3] :—"We make mention also of the Seraphim, whom Isaiah, by the Holy Ghost, beheld encircling the throne of God, and with two of their wings veiling their countenances, and with two their feet, and with two flying, who cried, 'Holy, Holy, Holy, Lord God of Sabaoth.' [Isa. vi. 1. Rev. iv. 8.] For this cause, therefore, we rehearse this confession of God, delivered down to us from the Seraphim, that we may join in hymns with the hosts of the world above."

The only part of "*It is very meet, right,*" &c., in which the choir and congregation should join, is the "Sanctus" itself. It has been the constant practice of the Church from the earliest times for the Priest alone to say the PREFACE, which in our Liturgy ends with the words "*evermore praising Thee and saying,*" and then for the people to take up the words "*Holy, holy, holy,*" with a solemn outburst of devout song, in which an Act of Divine Worship is performed by them as a part of the whole Communion of Saints. For "ye are come unto Mount Sion, and unto the City of the living God, the heavenly Jerusalem, and to an innumerable company of angels, to the general assembly and Church of the First-Born, which are written in Heaven, and to God the Judge of all, and to the spirits of just men made perfect." [Heb. xii. 22, 23.] And in this Communion with God, the Holy Angels, the Saints departed, and the Church on earth, this great act of the Celebrant and all others then present is performed.

There are " PROPER PREFACES" for the Priest to

Laity not to say, "Therefore with angels," &c.

---

[6] That is, the hymn "*Thrice Holy.*"

insert between the words "Everlasting God" and "Therefore with angels," at the four principal seasons, namely, *Christmas, Easter, Ascension,* and *Whitsuntide.* These Proper Prefaces are to be said on every day during the octave of the Festivals, and a fifth special one is appointed for Trinity Sunday, which is the last day of the Whitsun octave, and itself a Festival.

THE PRAYER OF HUMBLE ACCESS follows this great Act of Praise. It used formerly to be said after the Prayer of Consecration, and before the Communion, but has occupied its present position since 1552. It now forms a lowly approach of Priest and People to both the Act of Sacrifice and the Act of Communion ; and the name by which it is known in the Eastern Church, "The Prayer of bowing down," indicates the spirit with which that approach should be made.

THE CONSECRATION PRAYER was formerly the central portion of one long prayer, the first part of which is represented by the Prayer for the Church now said at the Offertory, and the latter part by the first Thanksgiving used after Communion

The object of Consecration is, that the Bread and Wine which have been offered and dedi- The purpose of cated to Almighty God in the Offertory Consecration. may become the "most blessed Body and Blood" of our Lord Jesus Christ, which being solemnly offered up to the Father as a sacrifice in memorial of Christ's Death and Passion, are then given to the communicants to be their "spiritual Food and Sustenance."

The Consecration is effected by the Priest or Bishop reciting the words and using the actions enjoined, which are those used and instituted by our Blessed Lord

This is the most solemn part of the whole Service.

The celebrant's position and work Standing at the head of the people in front of the Lord's Table, the earthly Priest stands there as the representative of the High Priest and Chief Shepherd whose deputy he is, to act in His name and by His authority. That which this earthly Priest does, is to use those ordained words and gestures by which "the outward part or sign," the elements of Bread and Wine, become united to "the inward part or thing signified, the Body and Blood of Christ[7]." In doing this he offers up a Memorial before the Father of the Sacrifice once for all effected upon the Cross, and for ever pleaded before the Throne, by the Lamb of GOD Himself. His words

The people's work. and acts are adopted by the congregation in the "Amen" which they say at the conclusion of the Prayer; and they are ratified by

Christ's work. Christ, Who becomes really present under the form of the outward signs, and thus associates them with His Body in Heaven.

Little or nothing can be said in explanation of this great mystery; and we must receive it humbly as a truth given us to believe, but not yet given us to understand. Believing the *fact* of Christ's "Real Presence," we can, however, understand that the result must be that of bringing Him nearer to us than at any other

Adoration of Christ, now present. time; and that while He is thus near to us we ought to be very humble and devout in all our gestures, thoughts, and words, adoring Him Whose Body and Blood are those of the Man Who is GOD.

Prayer to Christ, now present. If, moreover, we have any special prayers to offer up for the Church at large, for our friends on earth or in Para-

[7] See the Catechism.

dise, or for ourselves, this is the time when we may
well believe they will most surely come before Him,
whether or not it is His will to grant them.

§ 5. *The Communion.*

AFTER the Celebrant has administered " the Body and
Blood of Christ" to himself, he delivers them to the
Bishops, Priests, and Deacons who are officially present.
Then, in well-regulated churches, the other communicants receive in successive order, first the choir, as
subordinate " ministers " in the Service, then the men,
and lastly the women.

THE WORDS OF ADMINISTRATION are partly ancient and partly of the Reformation period. The
ancient portion ends at "everlasting life," and is
traceable to the early ages of the Church. The second
portion was *substituted* for these ancient words in
1552, but *added* to them as we now find it, in 1559.
The omission of the ancient words led some persons
to suppose that the Church of England had ceased to
recognize the Real Presence of our Lord; and by their
restoration each communicant is separately reminded
that what he receives is " The Body of our Lord Jesus
Christ, which was given for thee," and " The Blood of
our Lord Jesus Christ, which was shed for Thee;" so
that no excuse is left for ignorant unbelief.

The greatest reverence should be shown Mode of
in receiving this holy Sacrament. It has receiving.
been customary from the time of the Primitive Church
to place one open hand upon the other for the reception of the consecrated Bread, and to say " Amen "
after the words of Administration.

F

§ 6. *The Thanksgiving.*

WHEN all have received, the remains of the consecrated elements are covered with a veil,
that is, a " fair " or beautiful " linen cloth,"
in reverent token that they are as much the
Body and Blood of Christ when standing
upon the altar after Communion, as when they were
being administered to the communicants.

*Why the con-
secrated ele-
ments are
covered.*

THE LORD'S PRAYER which follows is used partly
as an act of Oblation, and partly as an act of Thanksgiving. In nearly all the ancient Liturgies, and in
that of the Church of England until 1552, it was said
before the reception of the consecrated elements instead of after ; but in its present position its thanksgiving office is more distinctly brought out. The repetition of it by the people as well as by the Priest, is a
practice of the Primitive Church maintained by the
Eastern and the English Churches in common.

THE PRAYER OF OBLATION is substantially taken
from that of the ancient Church of England, in which
it was said after Consecration, and before the Lord's
Prayer. It continues the act of Sacrifice[8], confirming
it with a definite petition to the Father that He will
accept that which has been offered. At this most
solemn time also, it makes, in the name of the congregation, an act of Re-dedication of each one, *now united
to Christ afresh*, as a reasonable, holy, and living
sacrifice. And it concludes with a petition that, not-

[8] The words "our sacrifice of praise and thanksgiving,"
are an English rendering of the ecclesiastical Greek word
" Eucharist."

withstanding our unworthiness to offer any sacrifice at all, God will accept this one,—that of the holy Eucharist, and of ourselves with whom Christ is now indwelling,—as our bounden duty and service. It is also observable that the "whole Church" is here prayed for ; which expression such holy men as Bishops Andrewes and Cosin have always considered to include the departed as well as the living members of it : for they, as well as we, are receiving the "benefits of His passion."

THE THANKSGIVING was very probably intended originally to be used after Communion, because the Prayer of Oblation had been used before : such having been the habit of Bishop Overall and other great Divines. The restoration of this custom is very much to be desired, as the two prayers are plainly constructed for these two distinct objects.

THE GLORIA IN EXCELSIS (which title is the beginning of the hymn as it used to be sung in Latin) is one of the oldest hymns of the Church. The most ancient copy of it known is in a Greek Bible of the fourth century, called "The Alexandrine Codex," which is preserved in the British Museum. It was anciently used at the beginning of the Communion Service, and was placed here in 1552. This is a change which has added greatly to the beauty and the meaning of the Liturgy ; for the Gloria in Excelsis is thus associated with the Sacrifice as an act of Worship, and with the Communion as an act of Thanksgiving.

THE BENEDICTION is a beautiful peculiarity of the English Office, though founded on two very ancient forms, the second of which, and probably the first also, was used in Anglo-Saxon times. It is a noble sequence to the doctrinal hymn just sung ; and sends forth those who have been brought so near to their Lord, with that peace of His Presence of which He said to His Church as His Steward, " My Peace I leave with you."

CHAPTER VII

𝕳𝖔𝖑𝖞 𝕭𝖆𝖕𝖙𝖎𝖘𝖒

" Go ye therefore, and teach all nations, baptizing them in the Name of the Father, and of the Son, and of the Holy Ghost."—MATT. xxviii. 19.

THE Baptismal Office of the Church of England was translated without much altera- History of the Office. tion for the Prayer Book of 1549, but considerable changes were made in the revision of 1552. Before the Reformation, the Service was still substantially in the form in which it had been handed down from the Primitive Church, when it had consisted of three separate Offices—the Admission of Catechumens (that is, those who had been prepared for Holy Baptism), the Benediction of the Font, and the Baptism itself. These three Offices had originally been used at separate times ; and, when they were joined together, and said at one time, the Service became long and complicated. Much popular superstition had also grown up around some of the ancient ceremonies used in Baptism ; and it was found desirable to leave some of them out of the Rubrics ; retaining firmly, however, the signing of the baptized with the Sign of the Cross.

But though these changes were made, the essential

Form of Baptism remained exactly the same as it had come down from the Primitive Church ; and most of the prayers now used are taken from the ancient Service.

As in the case of the Communion Service, this also may be best understood by dividing it into the several sections of which it is made up, these being (1) The Introduction, (2) The Baptismal Vows, (3) The Benediction of the Water, (4) The Baptism, (5) The Signing with the Cross, and (6) The Thanksgiving.

Its structure.

§ 1. *The Introduction.*

THE first portion of the Service, from its beginning to the end of the Collect, " Almighty and everlasting God, heavenly Father," answers to the ancient Service for the Admission of a Catechumen, which has been previously mentioned.

THE RUBRICS which follow the Title of the Office for the Public Baptism of Infants, are of much importance. The first relates to the expediency of administering Baptism *in public*, and its old form well explains why this is expedient.

Baptism to be public

"It appeareth by ancient writers, that the Sacrament of Baptism in the old time was not commonly ministered but at two times in the year, at Easter and Whitsuntide ; at which times it was openly ministered in the presence of all the congregation · which custom (now being grown out of use), although it cannot for many considerations be well restored again, yet it is thought good to follow the same as near as conveniently may be. Wherefore the people are to be admonished, that it is most convenient that Baptism should not be ministered but upon Sundays and other holy-days, when the most number of people may come together · as well for that the congregation there present may testify the receiving

of them that be newly baptized into the number of Christ's
Church ; as also because in the baptism of infants every man
present may be put in remembrance of his own profession
made to God in his baptism.   For which cause also it is
expedient that baptism be ministered in the English tongue.
Nevertheless (if necessity so require), children ought at all
times to be baptized either at the Church or else at home."

The necessity for Baptism is so great, that, in fact,
no time can be improper for making a child the child
of God ; but this rule of expediency respecting *Public*
Baptism is one that dates from the earliest age of
Christianity, and ought to be attended to by parents
as well as by the Clergy.   It is provided by the 68th
Canon that " No Minister shall refuse or delay to
christen any child according to the form of the Book
of Common Prayer that is brought to the Church to
him upon Sundays or Holy Days to be christened :
. . . . . convenient warning being given him thereof
before."   The " form of the Book of Common Prayer "
does not, however, allow of Baptisms in Church, except
after the Second Lesson—that is, in public, when the
congregation is present ; and (if necessity so require)
they may be so administered on any day, provided
they are administered at this part of Morning or
Evening Prayer.

The second of these introductory Rubrics Sponsors are
relates to the Sponsors, ordering that required.
every male child shall have two Godfathers and one
Godmother, and every female child one Godfather
and two Godmothers.   In the Eastern and the Latin
Churches only one sponsor is required, though two
are permitted.   In the Mediæval English Church
the number required was three, as by the present
Rubric.   The 29th Canon forbids the reception of the

parents of the child as its sponsors, for they are in fact its sponsors by their natural relation to it, and that in the *very highest degree;* but an attempt has been made legally to repeal this restriction, and it has received so much ecclesiastical authority, (having been confirmed by the Convocations of Canterbury and York,) that the restriction may be considered as practically removed.

The third Rubric requires notice of Baptisms to be
What notice to given to the Clergyman over-night, or in
be given. the morning before the beginning of Morning Prayer. The particulars to be given may be shown by the ancient Rubric, which required that when the child was brought for Baptism, the Priest should ask the nurse three questions, (1) Whether the child were a boy or a girl? (2) Whether it had been privately baptized? (3) What was intended to be the child's name? Much confusion would be avoided if the notice was always given in writing, with answers to these three questions, as they are often answered in Church in so low a voice, that there is a probability of mistakes arising, especially when the Clergyman's hearing is not quick.

Re-baptism The question, *"Hath this Child been*
improper *already baptized?"* is a very important one; as it is the unvarying doctrine of the Church, that a person once baptized cannot be baptized again - so that the use of the Form of Baptism over a Christian child could be only a pretence, irreverent even when
Conditional inadvertent, and sinful if intentional.
Baptism Should the child have been baptized by a Dissenting Preacher or any other Lay person, the Clergyman may consider it safest to use the Conditional Form, "If thou art not already baptized, I

baptize thee," unless he can be clearly satisfied that
the proper "matter" or material, which is Water, was
effectively used, and also the proper "Form," as set
down in the Prayer Book. Questions to be asked on
this subject are printed at the beginning of the Office
for the Private Baptism of Children.

THE ADDRESS, "Dearly Beloved," &c., is similar in
character to one which was used in the primitive
Churches of France, Spain, and England, but it does
not appear that any such address was used in Mediæval times. It very distinctly sets forth the object
for which children are baptized : that, being "con-
ceived and born in sin," they require to be "born anew
of Water and the Holy Ghost" before they can become members of Christ's Holy Church ; that is,
before they can become Christians.

THE TWO COLLECTS which follow are both ancient.
The first comes to us from an old German Baptismal
Office, through the German translation set forth by
Luther in 1523 : the second is from the ancient
English Office, and was associated with a Form of
Exorcism, by which Satan was bidden to depart from
the child to be baptized. This exorcism was adopted
in the Baptismal Office of 1549, but dropped at its
revision in 1552. While these Collects are being said,
the people should kneel ; the Priest standing throughout the Service, as a sign of authority, and that he acts
in the name of his Master.

THE GOSPEL ought to be preceded by the versicle
"Glory be to Thee, O Lord," and followed by "Thanks
be to Thee, O Lord," if such is the custom at the Holy
Communion. This Gospel was substituted for Matt. xix.
13—15, in 1549, as more distinctly showing the Divine
witness against those Anabaptist errors which infected

the Churches of Europe at that time, and which (as taught by the so-called "Baptists") still destroy thousands of souls for whom Christ died, and for whom, in His great love, He instituted Burial into His Death by Baptism, that they might be saved.

THE EXHORTATION is a short Homily on the Gospel. In its original form it ended with the saying of the Lord's Prayer and the Creed by all present; and the former is still enjoined in the Public Office which follows Private Baptism.

THE COLLECT following concludes the Introduction, and is substantially founded on the words of the Exhortation, praying God to grant that which it has just been declared that He is willing to give. There is no proper authority for the repetition of this Collect by the people; but the custom has probably arisen from that just mentioned, of their repeating the Lord's Prayer and Belief at this part of the Service

§ 2. *The Baptismal Vows.*

THE earliest Christian writings, and even the Holy Baptismal interrogatories. Scriptures, show that some form of interrogation always preceded Baptism. When the eunuch desired baptism from Philip the Deacon, the latter said, "If thou believest with all thine heart, thou mayest. And he answered and said, I believe that Jesus Christ is the Son of God." (Acts viii. 37.) It has also been commonly believed by sound interpreters, that St. Paul's words to Timothy, "Fight the good fight of faith, lay hold on eternal life, whereunto thou art also called, and hast professed a good profession before many witnesses" (1 Tim. vi. 12), refer to this custom. There is abundant evidence that interrogatories similar to those now in use were used in the Primitive Church ; and no doubt the custom is of Apostolic origin. Those of our Office relate to (1) the Vow of Renunciation, (2) the Vow of Belief, (3) the Vow of Obedience.

THE VOW OF RENUNCIATION is spoken of by the early Christian writers, and in the time of St. Cyril of Jerusalem (A.D. 315—386) it was made in the form " I renounce thee, Satan, and all thy works, and all thy pomp, and all thy service," the person making it turning to the West, and stretching out the right arm, as though actually speaking to the Evil One. This vow shows how keen a sense the Christian should have (1) of the actual existence of the Evil One, (2) of his power over mankind, and (3) of the utter impossibility of serving both Christ and Christ's Enemy.

THE VOW OF BELIEF is a profession of faith made in the words of the Apostle's Creed. In the Catechism, this Creed is spoken of as containing "all the Articles of the Christian Faith," which words illustrate the meaning of the question, "Wilt thou be baptized in this Faith?"

The profession of faith is founded on our Lord's words in Matt. xxviii. 19 ; and, from the case of the eunuch in Acts viii. 37, it appears to have been required from the very first. It seems also to be required by our Lord's words, " He that *believeth* and is baptized" (Mark xvi. 16) ; for as belief must necessarily, in adults, precede Baptism, so some confession of what is believed seems necessary as an outward evidence of belief. The object, however, is not that each person should declare his own private belief, but that he should assent to that of the Church. As regards the child, of course it is a promise in his name ;

and the declaration " All this I stedfastly believe," is, as regards the person speaking, identical with the " I believe" of the Creed which he is continually repeating in Divine Service.

THE VOW OF OBEDIENCE was not represented in the ancient Office, but was inserted here in 1661, probably because there were then many " Antinomians," who thought that a converted person was not bound to obey the law of God, being ever after conversion sure of salvation, come what might. For fear such a construction should be put by ignorant persons on the doctrine of new birth in Baptism, a declaration that constant obedience to the law of God is necessary for all Christians was embodied in this promise or vow.

§ 3. *The Benediction of the Water.*

THIS was formerly a separate service, as in the Primitive and Mediæval Church; consisting, in 1549, Principally of the four short prayers and the Collect now in use (which come down to us from very ancient times), and used once a month. In 1552 the Benediction of the Water was directed to be used at every Baptism, and the Office for it was incorporated with that of the Baptism itself. This benediction of the water of Baptism is not essential to the regeneration of the baptized person, as the pouring of the water upon him is; but it is a solemn recognition of the work of God in the Sacrament : a significant symbol of the Creator laying " the beams of His chambers"—the Temple of Christ's mystical body—" in the waters ;" of the Spirit of God moving upon the face of the waters for the purpose of new creation ; of the Victor breaking in pieces the head of the dragon in those waters, by means of which

the power of the Evil One is counteracted and defeated.
Being a rite of so solemn a kind, it should be performed
with reverence and exactness ; and so the old custom
of making the sign of the Cross in the water at the
word "sanctify," is very generally adopted, though it
is not now the practice to print the cross in the Prayer
Book, as formerly, in the places where it is proper to
use it. Care must also be taken that the benediction
is not repeated ; and, to avoid this, the water should be
let off from the font after the conclusion of the Baptismal Office.

It must be understood that the Benediction of the
Water sets it apart for a holy purpose, but does not
effect any spiritual change whatever in the water itself.

§ 4. *The Baptism.*

ALL that goes before is a preparation for the few
words and the simple act by which the Importance of
actual Baptism of the child is effected ; the act of
and all that follows is either thanksgiving Baptism.
for its regeneration, or exhortation arising out of it.
But those few words and that simple act are the means
by which original sin is removed, spiritual life given,
the foundation of holy living laid, and the capacity for
eternal life bestowed. Their importance cannot, therefore, be overrated ; too great exactness cannot be shown
by the Clergy in using them ; nor can the Laity be too
careful in all which depends upon them towards the
same object.

The Rubric directs the Priest to dip the infant in the
water discreetly and warily "*if the spon-* Baptism by
sors certify him that the child may endure immersion.
it . . . . but if they certify that the child is weak, it

shall suffice to pour water upon it" The sponsors
rarely, if ever, certify that the child may endure dip-
ping , and the fact of their bringing it to the font
fully clothed is, practically, certifying the contrary.
Probably there are few infants, with our modern habits,
who could be safely dipped in the water at any time of
the year, and certainly not in the winter ; so immersion has long ceased to be the ordinary method of
baptizing, in the Churches of Northern Europe at
least[1].

The practice substituted is shown by the words "*it*
Baptism by   *shall suffice to pour water upon it :*" and
affusion   this can be done most effectually by the
Priest pouring it from his hand or from a shell over
the *top of the child's head* as it lies on his *left* arm.
The infant's cap should therefore be removed, the head
fully exposed, and the infant so handed to the Priest
that he may without difficulty take it on his *left* arm.
Such care will prevent much confusion and embarras-
ment on the part of the Priest and sponsors, and much
crying on the part of the infants, who are rarely startled
when the cold water is poured on their heads, but
seldom otherwise when it is poured or sprinkled on
their faces. The more water used, the better.

§ 5. *The Signing with the Cross*

THIS is not an essential part of Holy Baptism, which
would be complete without it ; but it is a very meaning ceremony, which has come down to us from
The cross   the earliest ages of Christianity   In
anciently signed ancient days, and until the revision of
with oil   1552, the sign of the Cross was made with

[1] The Council of Trent speaks of pouring, or "affusion,"
as the "general practice" at that time, in the middle of the
sixteenth century.

unction, such as was used in Confirmation and Ordination, and such as is still used for signing the Cross on
our Sovereigns at their Coronation. The use of anoint-
ing oil has been discontinued, but that of the Cross
has been retained in the face of all the wicked opposition that was raised against it by the Puritans ; and a
long defence of the custom was drawn up in 1603,
which forms Canon 30 of the Canons set forth for the
Church of England in that year.

The words used by the Priest while signing the child
with the Cross are often misinterpreted, Declaration of
as if *by them* the child was received into the child's new
the Church.   It has been already received birth.
by the act of Baptism, which has made it a member of
Christ, a child of God, and an inheritor of the Kingdom of Heaven.   All that the Priest does by using
these words, is to *pronounce* that the infant is now one
of Christ's flock ; and, having done that, to make the
sign of the Cross on its forehead, in token that he is
enlisted under that Banner of Christ, manfully to fight
against Christ's enemies and to be His "faithful soldier
and servant unto his life's end."

Some of the wise words of the long Canon referred to
make this very clear.   "It is apparent," it says, "that
the infant baptized is, by virtue of Baptism, before it be
signed with the Sign of the Cross, received into the congregation of Christ's flock, as a perfect member thereof,
and not by any power ascribed unto the Sign of the
Cross. So that, for the very remembrance of the Cross,
which is very precious to all them that rightly believe in
Jesus Christ, and in the other respects mentioned, the
Church of England hath retained still the Sign of it in
Baptism ; following therein the Primitive and Apostolical Churches, and accounting it a lawful outward cere-

mony and honourable badge, whereby the infant is
dedicated to the service of Him that died upon the
Cross, as by the words used in the Book of Common
Prayer it may appear."

§ 6. *The Thanksgiving.*

THE short Address which immediately follows the
signing of the Cross, shows that THE LORD'S PRAYER
and THE COLLECT are to be used (1) as an act of
thanksgiving for the child's regeneration, and (2) as
an act of intercession for its final perseverance in the
way of salvation : the use of the Lord's Prayer in this
place being similar to its use after the Communion in
the Eucharistic Service. And when the Church bids us
" with one accord to make our prayers " to God, in the
very words of our Blessed Lord, it is with the obvious
intention of making that prayer the central point of
devotional expression and devotional unity ; a prayer
as capable of expressing with one accord the highest
praise and thanksgiving, as it is of expressing the
deepest penitence and humiliation.

Of the Collect which follows, it need only be re-
marked that it shows an unhesitating faith in the
effects of Holy Baptism ; and, also, an unhesitating
conviction that, without final perseverance on the part
of those who have been baptized and have afterwards
come to years of discrimination between good and evil,
there is no hope of the attainment of that everlasting
kingdom of which their regeneration has made them
heirs.

At the revision of 1661 the Presbyterians objected to
this Act of Thanksgiving after Baptism,—" We cannot
in faith say that every child that is baptized is 'regenerated by God's Holy Spirit;' at least it is a disput-

able point, and therefore we desire it to be otherwise expressed." To this the Bishops replied as follows,—having previously referred to John iii. and Acts iii. 3, for proof that "Baptism is our spiritual regeneration," and that by it "is received remission of sins :"—"Seeing that God's Sacraments have their effects, where the receiver doth not 'ponere obicem,' put any bar against them (which children cannot do) ; we may say in faith of every child that is baptized, that it is regenerated by God's Holy Spirit ; and the denial of it tends to Anabaptism, and the contempt of this holy Sacrament, as nothing worthy, nor material whether it be administered to children or not." Although this objection and its answer are contained in few words, they represent the substance of a long controversy, and the decision of the Church of England ; a decision deliberately expressed, and in the most solemn way, by words spoken to Almighty God, in this prayer.

PRIVATE BAPTISM.

THE Sacrament of Baptism is so "generally necessary for salvation," that a provision is made for christening children at home if they are dangerously ill, rather than they should be suffered to die without being "brought to Christ."

If a Priest or Deacon cannot possibly be procured for this purpose in time, some man[2] (or, if a man cannot be procured, a woman) should carefully pour water on the child, so as to be sure that it actually

[2] A lay *Churchman* should do this, rather than a Dissenting Preacher ; the former being a Layman in communion with the Church, the latter a Layman in schismatical separation from it. But either is a "lawful Minister" of Baptism in a case of such urgent necessity.

G

touches its person, saying *at the same time* the words
" John" (or " Mary," or whatever the name given may
be) " I baptize thee In the Name of the Father, and of
the Son, and of the Holy Ghost."

But no Laypersons should administer Baptism, except
in case of extreme necessity ; and when compelled to
do it, to save the child from dying unregenerate, they
should afterwards offer a prayer to God that their
act may be pardoned if it has been done presump-
tuously.

Whether a child has been privately baptized by a
Clergyman or by a Lay person, it should be taken to
Church for the appointed Service as soon as possible,
if it recovers. The object of that Service is (1) to make
a solemn public recognition of the child's regenerated
condition ; and (2) that the child may, by its sureties,
make those solemn engagements of the Baptismal Vow
which were omitted when it was thought that it would
never come of age to fulfil them.

ADULT BAPTISM.

THIS Service was introduced into the Prayer Book
in 1661, partly because so many persons had grown up
unbaptized in the profligate times of the Great Rebellion and Persecution, and partly to provide for the
baptism of converts from heathenism in our foreign
dominions. It is substantially the same as the Service
for baptizing Infants ; but the persons to be baptized
are required to answer for themselves instead of by
their Godfathers and Godmothers. They must be
well instructed before being baptized.

CHAPTER VIII

Confirmation

" The God of all grace, Who hath called us unto His eternal glory by Christ Jesus . . . make you perfect, stablish, strengthen, settle you."—1 PET. v. 10.

THE notice which concludes the Service for the Baptism of Infants is as follows :—

"Ye are to take care that *this child* be brought to the Bishop to be confirmed by him, so soon as *he* can say the Creed, the Lord's Prayer, and the Ten Commandments, in the vulgar tongue, and be further instructed in the Church Catechism set forth for that purpose."

This shows the intention of the Church, as regards the spiritual progress of Christians in their early days. It is, that as soon as they come to an age when they are capable
Catechizing before Confirmation.
of learning, they shall be instructed in the principles of Faith, Prayer, and Obedience to God, according to the tenour of the Vows made in their name. For this purpose the Church Catechism is set forth as a concise and easily-learned system of Christian doctrine. When this has been well learned, both as to words and meaning, the child is to be brought to the Bishop for

G 2

Confirmation; and no age is any where mentioned
Age not laid   in the Prayer Book or other rules of the
down.   Church. According to the modern capacity of children, they are able to learn what is required
by the time they are from ten to twelve years old ;
but if they are quick and intelligent children, they will
probably be ready to " be brought to the Bishop to be
confirmed by him " at an even earlier age.

The *object of Confirmation* is well stated in the old
Rubric out of which the modern " Preface " read at the
beginning of the Service was formed. " . . . . . Confirmation is ministered to them that be baptized, that, by
imposition of hands and prayer, they may receive
strength and defence against all temptations to sin,
and the assaults of the world and the devil   it is most
meet to be ministered when children come to that age,
that, partly by the frailty of their own flesh, partly by
the assaults of the world and the devil, they begin to
be in danger to fall into sin."

THE CATECHIZING at Confirmation formerly consisted in an actual repetition by the Candidates of the
                Church Catechism, or of so much of it as
Obligations of the Bishop or his deputy might think fit
Baptism pub-
licly accepted to ask. But in 1661 the question, " *Do*
before Con-
firmation.   *ye here,*" &c., was substituted for the
                Catechism itself, each parish Clergyman
being presumed to have previously instructed his
Candidates in the latter. The short answer, " I DO,"
taken in connexion with the question to which it is a
reply, contains, as has been already shown, an implicit
renewal of the Baptismal Vows ; and is a repetition,
under more solemn circumstances, and to God's chief
Minister, of the answer in the Catechism, "Yes, verily;
and by God's help so I will," to the question. " Dost

thou not think that thou art bound to believe, and to do, as they have promised for thee?" The connexion of this latter solemn adjuration with the "I do" of the Confirmation Service is accidentally indicated by the first versicle, "Our help is in the Name of the Lord." Every time the answer in the Catechism has been repeated by the children catechized, they have ratified and confirmed in their own persons, and acknowledged themselves bound to believe and to do, all those things which their Godfathers and Godmothers undertook for them, i. e. promised on their behalf, at their Baptism. They now ratify and confirm those Baptismal Vows in as solemn a manner as possible, not before their parish Priest only, but before the Bishop, who is the highest spiritual officer of Christ on earth, and His chief ministerial representative. This preliminary catechizing is therefore a formality of a very significant character, and, although no essential part of the rite of Confirmation, is a preparation for it which ought not to be passed over lightly. It marks the last step in the pathway of Christian childhood; and, on the verge of Christian maturity, sounds the trumpet-call of Christian duty to those who have promised manfully to fight under Christ's banner against sin, the world, and the devil, and to continue His faithful soldiers and servants unto their lives' end. The last stone in the foundation of the Christian life is about to be laid, and sealed with God's signet in confirmation of His promises. It is a time to remember, that although "the foundation of God standeth sure, having this seal, The Lord knoweth them that are His," there is a "reverse" as well as an "obverse" to the seal of Confirmation; and that it has another inscription, "Let every one that nameth the Name of Christ depart from iniquity"

(2 Tim. ii 19). The new blessing confirms the promise of God made in Baptism; it also enforces again that obligation of faithful service, from which the Christian can never become free.

THE PRAYERS consist of six short *versicles* and a Collect. Both of these were used in the Primitive Church, and in the Mediæval Church of England; but the versicles are all taken from the Psalms. The Collect is known to have been used in the Confirmation Office of the Church of England for at least 1150 years, or since A.D. 700, at which date it is found in an Office-book used by Egbert, Archbishop of York, as if it was the established form familiar to the Bishops of that early age. The sense and application of this Collect may be well shown by the objection raised against it by the Puritans in 1661, and the answer made by the Bishops. "This supposeth," said the former, "that all the children who are brought to be confirmed have the Spirit of Christ, and the forgiveness of all their sins; whereas a great number of children at that age, having committed many sins since their baptism, do show no evidence of serious repentance, or of any special saving grace; and therefore this Confirmation (if administered to such) would be a perilous and gross abuse." This was a reverent objection, but showed considerable ignorance of the theological principles on which the Offices of the Church are framed, as well as of the manner in which they are intended to be administered. The reply of the Bishops was short, but pointed and consistent with the principles of the Prayer Book. "It supposeth, and that truly, that all children were at their baptism regenerate by water and the Holy Ghost, and had given unto them the forgiveness of all their sins; and it is charitably presumed that, notwithstanding the frailties and slips of their childhood, they have not totally lost what was in Baptism conferred upon them; and therefore adds, 'Strengthen them, we beseech Thee, O Lord, with the Holy Ghost the Comforter, and daily increase in them Thy manifold gifts of grace,' &c. None that lives in open sin ought to be confirmed."

THE ACT OF CONFIRMATION is performed by the Bishop laying his hand or hands on the head of each person to be confirmed. It _{Mode of Confirmation.} was the ancient practice of the Church for the Bishop to make the Sign of the Cross, with unction, on the forehead of each person; and the first Prayer Book, of 1549, directed this practice to be continued, the Bishop using the words, "*N.* I sign thee with the Sign of the Cross, and lay my hand upon thee, In the Name of the Father, and of the Son, and of the Holy Ghost. Amen." The present Benediction was substituted in 1552, and is founded on the words of the preceding Collect. The act, that is, the Imposition of Hands, is the essential part of the rite of Confirmation, no words, and no other ceremony being absolutely necessary for conveying the grace given. Unction, however, had been used from the time of the Apostles, and probably it had always been used with the Sign of the Cross; so that its disuse was a great innovation upon the custom of the Church.

The Act of Confirmation is an outward sign of an inward grace, the latter being that gift of the Holy Spirit by which the person is established, or made *firm* in his position _{Sacramental character of the rite.} as a Christian, and strengthened for the duties of the Christian life. It is God's own preparation of a baptized child for the still greater gift bestowed in Holy

Communion ; and hence none are ordinarily to become communicants until they have been confirmed.

THE LORD'S PRAYER is used here, as after Communion and Baptism, in the sense of a thanksgiving for the great mercy vouchsafed by God in bestowing His grace. It was placed here in 1661, not being so used in the ancient Office.

THE COLLECT was composed for the first Prayer Book of 1549, but is similar to that of the ancient Office. The second Collect was inserted in 1661, being one of those printed at the end of the Communion Service.

THE BENEDICTION is that of the ancient Office ; but it was formerly preceded by the 5th and 6th verses of the 128th Psalm.

THE FINAL RUBRIC is founded on a Canon of the Church passed in the time of Archbishop Peckham, A.D. 1281, which ordered that " None shall be admitted to the Sacrament of the Body and Blood of Christ (except at the point of death) unless he has been confirmed, or has been reasonably hindered from receiving Confirmation."

There are sometimes cases in which a child or an adult, with the proper amount of knowledge respecting faith and duty, strongly desires Confirmation and the Holy Communion, but cannot obtain the former. The desire for Confirmation is then to be taken as satisfying the rule of the Church ; and the Holy Communion is not to be refused.

Arch, 1966, pp. 25-6, first

1, p. 23, 1 Feb. 1858.

that during the Georgian
Pusey as early advocates
1 Christ and with each
e ordering of the whole
the Eucharist as a sign of
gued that one of the aims
nvisaged as a Eucharistic
ionism, Joseph Arch. It
ory of the observer, the
; commencement of the
ural social hierarchy on
nobody knelt with them;
oor agricultural labourers
.. wheelwright, and the

CHAPTER IX

Holy Matrimony

" Whoso findeth a wife findeth a good thing, and obtaineth favour of the Lord."—PROV. xviii. **22.**

THE object of the Marriage Service is to unite man and wife together "in the Christian Lord," and to make their union such that Marriage. they can be declared to be "joined together by God."

Those persons who desire to live together as man and wife, without public disgrace, but not Legalized to be joined together by God in Holy cohabitation. Matrimony, go to the Registrar of Marriages, who makes their cohabitation legal by entering it in his Register-book[1].

"The Form of Solemnization of Matrimony" is derived from two ancient Offices. of the Origin of the Church of England, the one appointed Office. for the celebration of Espousals, the other for that of

[1] If persons so licensed to live together, afterwards desire to be "joined together by God," the Marriage Service can still be performed ; but no entry is to be made in the Register of Marriages unless a separate one is kept exclusively belonging to the Church, in which case it is to be entered in that alone.

Marriage. The former Service was used some time previously as a solemn sanction of the engagement or contract to marry at a future day ; and it appears that the former part of our present Service was used in the same manner up to the time when all things were unsettled by the approach of the great Rebellion. An engagement so contracted was considered almost as binding as marriage itself.

§ 1 *Banns of Marriage.*

SOME public notice of marriage has always been required by the Church, and the law of the Church of England strictly forbids any Clergyman to marry persons unless their "banns" have been asked in Church on three successive Sundays or Holy days, unless a licence (or dispensation from banns) has been procured from the Bishop, through his proper officer, the "surrogate" of the district.

No Clergyman can be required to publish banns of Marriage, unless a notice in writing is given to him seven days before the first publication, stating the names of the persons, their places of abode, and the time during which they have lived there. If the man and woman live in different parishes, the banns must be asked in both ; and, in whichever parish of the two the marriage takes place, a certificate of the due publication of banns must be obtained from the Clergyman of the other parish, and presented to the Clergyman of that in which the persons are to be married.

Seven days' notice of banns.

These rules are intended to prevent secret marriages, which have always been held in abhorrence by the Church, as likely to

Hours for Marriage.

promote sin. For the same reason, no marriage may be solemnized before eight o'clock in the morning, or after twelve at noon, without a special licence from the Archbishop of Canterbury.

Marriages have always been discouraged by the Church, and, indeed, forbidden, during Marriage the seasons of Advent and Lent, and from improper during Rogation Sunday to Trinity Sunday ; and Lent. all good Christians ought, at least, to avoid being married during the season of Lent.

§ 2. *The Espousal.*

THE first part of the Marriage Office, as far as the answers " I will," represents the ancient First part of Espousal; it and all up to the Psalm being Service in directed to be said in the body of the the Nave. Church, that is, in some part of the nave. Anciently, this part of the Service was said near the Church door, but now the ordinary place is the entrance of the chancel.

THE EXHORTATION, setting forth the objects of Marriage, represents a very ancient form of a similar kind that was used in the Mediæval Church of England, and probably in other Churches, and which is given at page 7. The solemn charge to make known any impediment is also of the same antiquity.

· The impediments of Marriage are chiefly " consanguinity" (relationship in blood), and Forbidden "affinity" (relationship by Marriage). A degrees. table of such relationships or " forbidden degrees" is often printed with Prayer Books and Bibles, and may be made clearer still as follows :—

1. *Relatives whom a Man may not Marry.*

Mother, or
Stepmother } of his own or his wife's parents.

Widow of {
his father, or father-in-law.
,, uncle.
,, brother.
,, son, or step-son.
,, nephew.

Aunt
Sister
Daughter, or
Niece } of himself or his wife.

Daughter, or
Step-daughter } of his own or his wife's children.

2. *Relatives whom a Woman may not Marry.*

Father, or
Step-father } of her own, or of her husband's, parents.

Widower of {
her mother, or mother-in-law.
,, aunt.
,, sister.
,, daughter, or step-daughter.
,, niece.

Uncle
Brother
Son, or
Nephew } of herself or her husband.

Son, or
Step-son } of her own, or of her husband's, children.

These "forbidden degrees" are founded on an express law of God, laid down by Him in Lev. xviii. 6—18 ; and observation shows that when they are disregarded, childlessness, or the inborn seeds of disease in the offspring, are the result—most frequently in the second generation.

THE MUTUAL CONSENT of the persons afterwards to be married is then solemnly given, by each replying "I will" to the question asked by the Priest. This is also given in its ancient form, at page 7. The mutual consent is no mere formality, but a form of open declaration before God and man, that the Marriage is willingly undertaken by each, and not *forced* upon either man or woman. It also constitutes a promise respecting the duties of Marriage ; and must be taken as being, in effect, a preliminary vow made before God. And it is to be observed that this vow is binding " as long as ye both shall live."

§ 3. *The Marriage.*

EACH being thus *espoused* to each other, the Minister asks, according to very ancient custom, " Who giveth this woman to be married to this man ?" Dependence Upon which the woman is delivered over of woman by her father or his representative, to the signified. Church, and by the Church (represented by the Priest) delivered over to her future husband. The " independence " of woman is not recognized by the law of God, and therefore not by the Church of God. The father's authority over her is delivered up to God Who gave it, and then transferred by God to the husband, who " is the head of the wife," and who, by Divine ordinance, is to " rule over ? her. Such follies as are talked of under the name of " woman's rights," are always associated with infidelity, and are contrary to the principles on which God has founded the relation of woman to man.

THE BETROTHAL, or " giving of troth" (that is, *fidelity* or *allegiance*) to each other, is the What constitutes next ceremony. Each alternately taking the Marriage the right hand of the other [2], says the Vow.

---

[2] There was a curious distinction in the ancient Rubric, that a maiden should give her right hand ungloved, but a widow with her glove on.

words of the very ancient Marriage Vow. The quaint and touching words of this vow express again, and in a still more comprehensive form, the obligations of the marriage state, which were previously expressed in the mutual consent. Each promises an undivided allegiance to the other, until the death of one or the other shall part them asunder. That is, as God joins them together, so His Providential dispensation alone is able *really* to break the link which is forged by

Relation of man and wife to each other. Marriage. On both sides a promise is given of love and support under all the circumstances of life, prosperous or adverse. The duties of support, shelter, and comfort, which ordinarily fall upon the husband chiefly, may, under some circumstances (though they rarely arise), fall chiefly upon the wife ; and if by sickness and infirmity he is unable to fulfil them towards her, he has a claim upon her, by these words, that she shall fulfil them towards him. Under any circumstances each promises to be a stay to the other, according to their respective positions and capacities, on their way through life. In the marriage vow of the woman the modern phrase " to obey" is substituted for the obsolete one " to be buxom," or " boughsome" (that is *pliant*), which had the same meaning. It implies that although the woman's dependence on and obedience to her father has been given up by him into God's hands, it is only that it may be given over to her husband. Since it pleased our Blessed Lord to make woman the instrument of His Incarnation, her condition has been far more honourable than it was before ; but part of that honour is that " the husband is the head of the wife, even as Christ is the Head of the Church." Natural instinct, good sense, mutual love, and, above

all, religious feeling, will always enable the wife to dis-
cern how far she is bound to obey, and the husband
how far it is his duty to rule ; and, regulated by these,
the yoke of obedience will never be one which the
woman need regret to wear, or wish to cast aside.
Jeremy Taylor has well pointed out that nothing is
said in the husband's part of the marriage vow about
" rule," for this is included in the word "love."   " The
dominion of a man over his wife is no other than as
the soul rules the body ; for which it takes a mighty
care, and uses it with a delicate tenderness, and cares
for it in all contingencies, and watches to keep it from
all evils, and studies to make for it fair provisions, and
very often is led by its inclinations and desires, and
does never contradict its appetites but when they are
evil, and then also not without some trouble and sorrow ; and its government comes only to this—it furnishes the body with light and understanding, and the
body furnishes the soul with hands and feet ; the soul
governs because the body cannot else be happy."   So
also he writes in respect to the obedience of the wife :
" When God commands us to love Him, He means we
should obey Him: 'this is love, that ye keep My commandments ;' and ' if ye love Me, keep My commandments.'   Now, as Christ is to the Church, so is the
man to the wife, and therefore obedience is the best
instance of her love, for it proclaims her submission,
her humility, her opinion of his wisdom, his pre-emi-
nence in the family, the right of his privilege, and the
injunction imposed by God upon her sex, that although
' in sorrow she bring forth children,' yet with ' love and
choice she should obey.'   The man's authority is love,
and the woman's love is obedience."

THE WEDDING-RING has been used from the

earliest ages in Christian marriages, but was probably adopted from the customs of the Jews and Heathens. Anciently, gold and silver were given with the ring, as symbols of the dowry with which the husband endowed his wife : and the whole custom seems like that of patriarchal days, when Abraham's steward betrothed Rebecca, on the part of Isaac, by putting "the ear-rings upon her face, and the bracelets upon her

Meaning of the ring. hands." The ring may be considered to mean two things : (1) that the wife is thus linked to the husband, and hence both to each other : and (2) that eternity, constancy, and integrity, true as gold, and unending as a ring, are the characteristics of the marriage bond.

The proper way for the man to give the ring to the

How to put it on woman, is to place it lightly on the thumb of the left hand at the words "of the Father," on the next finger at the words "of the Son," on the third finger at the words "of the Holy Ghost," and on the fourth finger, so that it may permanently remain there, at the word "Amen." Then he is to hold the ring in its final place, while the Priest says the following prayer, which represents the ancient benediction of the Ring.

THE JOINING OF HANDS and the accompanying

Sentence of Marriage. solemn declaration completes the Marriage so far, that it cannot henceforth be dissolved, except by Him who has (by His agent and deputy) effected it. The words, "Those whom God hath joined together, let no man put asunder," are the Lord's own words, and are here used distinctly and authoritatively in His name. No divorce, or "putting asunder by man," can break the *spiritual* union that has now been accomplished and declared, by the authority of Christ, and in the name of the Holy Trinity.

THE BENEDICTION in the same most holy Name completes that part of the Service which is to be said in the nave or body of the Church. It is translated from the ancient Latin form.

§ 4. *The Holy Communion.*

THE part of the Service which follows belongs properly to the celebration of a Marriage Eucharist; and it is begun by the Priest and Choir leading the way to the Altar, while they sing the INTROIT, or entrance to the Altar, Psalm. The first of the two appointed is the one ordinarily to be used; the second being intended for the marriage of old people, when there is no expectation of offspring.

THE LORD'S PRAYER, VERSICLES, COLLECTS, and BENEDICTION, which follow, are all taken from the ancient Latin Office. To combine them properly with the Communion Service, the latter should begin at the "Offertory" and "Prayer for the Church Militant," immediately after the Homily, "All ye that are married," or the Sermon substituted for it.

H

CHAPTER X

The Visitation of the Sick

*"Despise not thou the chastening of the Almighty · for He
maketh sore, and bindeth up. He woundeth, and His hands
make whole."*—JOB v. 17, 18.

THIS Office provides a formal rite, to be once used
over the sick person; and not to be used, either
Object of the wholly or piecemeal, as the ordinary
Office. prayers of the Clergyman in his frequent
pastoral visits. It is a solemn recognition of the
person over whom it is used as one in the fellowship of the Church, and for whom the Church, by its
authorized Minister, offers up prayer to God. It is
also a solemn acknowledgment before God that the
sicknesses and infirmities of life are the consequences
of sin—a part of that inheritance which comes upon
us from the Fall. It is strictly a Churchman's Office,
and would be very much out of place if used over
one who was separated from the communion of the
Church.

Nearly all the Rubrics and Prayers of this Office are
Origin of the to be found in the ancient Service Books
Office. of the Church of England, and some of
the Prayers can be traced to the times of the Primitive

Church. Where alterations or additions have been made (as in the Exhortations) the spirit of the original has been closely adhered to ; and the only great omissions are—(1) a procession of the Priest and Choir to the house of the sick person, singing the seven penitential Psalms ; and (2) the Service for Extreme Unction. The latter was provided for by the First Prayer Book ; but since 1552 its use has been left (as are his other ministrations to the sick) to the discretion of the Clergyman.

The Office for the Visitation of the Sick is one in which there are many responses ; there ought therefore to be some persons, as well as the sick person, present to say these responsive portions.

Should be said responsively.

§ 1. *The Prayers.*

AFTER THE SALUTATION—which is that enjoined on the Apostles by our Lord (Luke x. 5)—the Priest is immediately to proceed to the Prayers. The first of these is an ANTIPHON to the LORD'S PRAYER. The object of this Antiphon is to fix the sense in which the Prayer of our Lord is to be used, that sense being here a penitential one. Both the Antiphon and its Response, " Spare us, good Lord," are familiar to us in our present Litany. The VERSICLES which follow are taken from the 20th, the 61st, the 86th, and the 89th Psalms, and represent a strain of responsive supplication which has been ascending to the Throne of God for the sick during a long course of ages. The COLLECTS are also translated from the ancient Latin. The first of them is directed towards seeking comfort and help for the sick man from God, and gathers up the

H 2

petitions of the versicles which have gone before. The second sets forth sickness as an instrument in the hand of the Almighty for good, and prays that the present trial may be sanctified to the sufferer. The "accustomed goodness" of God is here invoked, not for the recovery of the patient, or even for support under trial, but that the Fatherly correction may work the end God has intended in sending it. If sickness is to answer any good end, it must be viewed as Fatherly correction; and, if it comes from our Father, to Him we may go for help and comfort under it, and we may be persuaded that it comes for some good purpose. Looking to God as Father, our own weakness will lead us more to Him, will make us feel our dependence on Him more; in short, will strengthen our faith. The sense of weakness will force on us the uncertainty of life, will make us remember how short our time is, and bring us to more earnest repentance for all we have done amiss, as remembering the account we may so soon have to give before our God. The prayer, too, reminds those who hear it, that the repentance and sorrow are not to be limited simply to a sick bed; but that in case of recovery the good work begun in time of affliction must be carried out. How necessary to pray, " If it shall be Thy good pleasure to restore him to his former health, he may lead the residue of his life in Thy fear"! How many are there who promise well when God's hand is upon them, who seem full of godly sorrow for sin, and Christian hatred of it, who yet on recovery forget all, and fall back into old sins, and form new evil habits!

And since the issues of life and death are with the Lord, and we know not what the event may be,—recovery or death,—the Collect prays, not only that in case of restoration the sick man may be enabled to live to God, but that in case his illness prove fatal, he may, through the grave and gate of death, pass to a joyful resurrection, and, this life ended, dwell for ever with God in life everlasting.

§ 2. *The Exhortation.*

THIS is founded on a very ancient English exhortation, entitled " How thou shalt comfort a man that he grucche nought when he is seke." It is, in fact, a short Homily on Hebrews xii. 6—10, and contains a valuable statement of the manner in which sickness ought to be regarded by a Christian. There are circumstances under which it may be very desirable, both for the sick person and for the Clergyman, that the words of exhortation should be the authorized words of the Church, rather than those of an individual Priest. But pastors thoroughly trained to their duties will bring out of their treasuries things new and old, and cannot be restricted, with advantage, to the homiletic addresses of a former age. Whether, however, the authorized homily, or any other address be used, it is to conclude with a rehearsal of the Apostles' Creed, that by the answer " All this I stedfastly believe," the sick person may make a " PROFESSION OF FAITH " in all the fundamental truths which make for salvation.

§ 3. *The Confession of Sins.*

MUCH of this Office is of an intercessory character, and the sick man himself may be supposed to join in it rather with the heart than with the voice. But the central portion of it is undoubtedly the "special Con-

fession of his sins," and the following Absolution. The
sick person will probably wish to make this special
confession in private, and others should therefore with-
draw out of hearing. Such a confession is the best
proof that can be given of real sorrow for sin and desire for pardon; and it is so sad for a soul to leave this
world with unrepented sin defiling it, that the Priest is
required to urge it upon him ·—" Here shall the sick
person be moved to make a special confession of his
sins, if he feel his conscience troubled with any weighty
matter;" and his conscience is sure to be troubled if there
is such " weighty matter" of sin upon it, unless it has
become seared and deadened.

The particular form in which " Special Confessions"
are to be made, is not laid down in the Prayer Book,
but the following is commonly used ·—" In the Name
of the Father, and of the Son, and of the Holy Ghost,
Amen. I confess to God the Father Almighty, to His
only-begotten Son Jesus Christ our Lord, to God the
Holy Ghost, and to you, father, that I have sinned
exceedingly in thought, word, and deed, through my
fault, through my most grievous fault. [Here comes
in a statement of the sins troubling the person's
conscience.] For these and all my other sins which
I cannot now remember, I humbly beg pardon of
Almighty God, and grace to amend; and of you, my
father, I ask penance, counsel, and absolution. And
therefore I beseech God the Father Almighty, His
only-begotten Son Jesus Christ, and God the Holy
Ghost, to have mercy upon me, and you, father, to
pray for me."

The ABSOLUTION which follows is the most complete and solemn form of Absolution enjoined by the
Church,—the Priest declaring " By His authority com-

mitted to me, I absolve thee from all thy sins, In the name of the Father, and of the Son, and of the Holy Ghost." If the Confession has been honest, true, and made with real penitence of heart, this Absolution conveys to the penitent the most entire pardon of sin that he can receive in this world. Whether it has been so made, God only can fully judge ; but the Priest must judge as well as he can, so as not to make a mockery of the Absolution by giving it to a person evidently impenitent [1].

The Absolution COLLECT, as that which follows the Absolution itself may very properly be called, is among the most ancient Forms of the Church of Christ, having been used for many ages in the Church of England, and being found in the Prayer Book of Gelasius, A.D. 494, where it is called " The Reconciliation of a Penitent in the Hour of Death." It seals with prayer the preceding word of Absolution, carrying it up with the penitent's Confession to the throne of Almighty God, and beseeching Him to accept and to confirm what has been offered to Him, and done in His name.

§ 4. *The Psalm.*

THIS Psalm, the 71st, is handed down from the ancient Office ; in which, however, the whole of it was used.

Christ Himself is here heard speaking, and thus putting words upon the lips of His sick servant. They

---

[1] Where the time is short, and death imminent, as in the case of many modern accidents, cholera, or after a battle, the best thing the dying man can do, will be at once to make this special Confession, in however few words ; and his best passport to the other world will be the Absolution of the Priest attending upon him.

are His words at the time when the voice of the Passion
had not yet given place to the voice of the Resurrection Victory ; and in them we hear the " patient abid-
ing alway" of the Holy Jesus, waiting God's good
pleasure, and never doubting the righteousness of the
Divine Will. Thus the greatest of all sufferers offers to
His suffering servants His own words, as well as His
own example ; and with Him they may say, " I will go
forth in the strength of the Lord God."

The following ANTIPHON, "O Saviour of the world,"
clearly points out the sense in which the Psalm to
which it is appended should be used, pleading the sufferings there expressed as the cause of that human
sympathy which is still, and ever will be, felt for His
members by the Divine Saviour. It is an exact translation of the Old Latin.

§ 5. *The Benedictions.*

THE first of these is formed from an ancient Collect
in St. Gregory's Visitation Office, A.D. 590. The second
is the ancient Benediction which God ordained, saying,
" On this wise ye shall bless the children of Israel '
(Numb vi 23, 26.) It appears in ancient Irish and
French Missals as far back as the seventh century, but
was placed in the English Visitation Office in 1661.

THE COMMUNION OF THE SICK.

IN the ancient Church of England, as in the modern
Latin and Eastern Churches, it was the custom to reserve a portion of the consecrated Bread in a receptacle
near the Altar, that it might be taken, if necessary, to
those who were unable from sickness to come to Church

and receive it. This practice was discontinued (as a rule) after 1552, and the present Collect, Epistle, and Gospel, with the accompanying Rubrics were provided, so that the Holy Communion might be celebrated, as well as administered, in the sick person's presence.

Reverent preparation should be made in the room of the sick person, that this may be done with proper solemnity. Every thing should be as clean and orderly as the circumstances of the case will permit ; and " a convenient place,"—a small table as much apart from mere domestic furniture as can be arranged,—should be provided as a temporary Lord's Table, where all things may be done decently and in order ; considering His honour, as well as the good of the sick person's soul.

CHAPTER XI

The Burial of the Dead

"I will lay me down in peace, and take my rest · for it is Thou, Lord, only, that makest me dwell in safety."— PSALM iv. 9.

THE Office for the Burial of the Dead is a Form for commending to the care of Almighty God the
Object of the Office. bodies and souls of those who have died in the Communion of Saints, and in the broad charity which runs through all the Offices of the Church of England, it is assumed that all have so died of whom the contrary is not clearly proved. But reverence towards God must be considered, as well as charity towards men ; and, accordingly, a rule is laid down forbidding the use of the office over those who have clearly *not* died in the Communion of Saints, and these are mentioned in the opening Rubric.

1. First of such unhappy persons, are the *unbaptized.*
Not to be used over any but Christians. There are many infants who are left un-christened through the carelessness or irreligion of parents, and who die in their infancy. There are also not a few who grow up to more mature life without Baptism, among the sect mis-called " Baptists," and die before the adult age when

alone that sect permits persons to be baptized. All these are, of course, included in the terms of the Rubric, and the use of the Burial Service over them is strictly forbidden[1].

2. Those who die " excommunicate " are the second class of persons excluded from the benefit of the Office ; but the formal sentence of excommunication is seldom given in the present day, and the Rubric does not refer to those upon whom it would be pronounced, if strict discipline *were* exercised. It sometimes happens that persons have died in a state of notorious sin, when even the utmost charity cannot believe in their repentance. Clergymen will be found to run the risk of prosecution and loss by treating these as excommunicated persons, and will refuse to say the Burial Service over them. And in such very extreme cases, sensible and right-thinking relatives will feel that the omission is right, however painful to their feelings.

Nor over excommunicated persons.

3. The Rubric also excludes those who "have laid violent hands upon themselves." Christian charity has always made some distinction between those who 'murder themselves, and those who have killed themselves while in a state of insanity ; but such a distinction is not made by the Rubric ; and it rests entirely on the judgment of the responsible Clergyman of the parish, whether the Ser-

Nor over self-murderers.

[1] The present Archbishop of Canterbury decided in a case of this kind (when some Unitarians complained to him of the Clergyman), " That the Service of the Church of England for the Burial of the Dead is intended for those who have been made members of the Church of Christ by baptism ; and that to use that Service over the unbaptized would be an anomalous and irregular proceeding on the part of a Minister of the Church of England."

vice shall be read over *any* suicide. He will always
give the verdict of the Coroner's jury his
respectful attention ; but it has become a
sort of *fashion* for juries to find verdicts
of " Temporary Insanity," without any
proof whatever of the insanity ; and it would be contrary to reason and common sense for him always to
be guided by it[2]. It is his bounden duty to refuse to
say the Burial Office over those who have clearly been
murderers of themselves, (1) That he may not profane
the sacred rite which he is entrusted to use, and
(2) Because its omission may have some effect in
preventing suicide. In such cases, as in those previously mentioned, the Clergyman ought to receive the
sorrowful support of the relatives in the course which
he is bound to take.

Verdict of " Temporary Insanity" not always true.

§ 1. *The Service in Church.*

IT is the solemn and beautiful habit of the Church
of England for the " Priest and Clerks " (that is, the
Choir, where there is one) to meet the funeral procession at the Churchyard gate, and thence to lead it
into the Church (or straight to the grave, when death
has resulted from an infectious disease) saying or
singing the PROCESSIONAL ANTHEM, " I am the Resurrection and the Life." The first two clauses of this
Anthem were used in the " Dirge," sung every evening
while the corpse lay unburied in ancient times ; and

---

[2] The "Coroner's warrant" only releases the body from
the custody of the Crown, and so *permits* the relatives to
bury it. In ordinary cases it can impose no obligation as to
interment ; but where the verdict is " *Felo de se*" it orders
the body to be buried in a churchyard or cemetery, without
any religious rite, between nine and twelve o'clock at night.

the last was added for our English Service. When in
the Church, the mourning yet hopeful strain is taken
up in the PSALMS, one or both of which are to be sung
or said, in accordance with a custom as old probably
as Christianity. From 1552 to 1661 no Psalms were
used in the Burial Service ; but they were happily
restored at the latter date, and thus the Office regained
its ancient and primitive character. The LESSON is
one of the portions of Scripture which has been recognized in connexion with the Burial of the Dead
since the time of St. Jerome, A.D. 345—420 ; and it is
wisely chosen for the purpose, since it so clearly sets
forth the doctrine of our Lord's Incarnation as the
source of all spiritual life in this world or the next.

If the HOLY COMMUNION is celebrated at a Funeral,
the proper time for it is immediately after the Lesson,
while the body of the deceased is still in the Church.
The custom, recently revived, is one of primitive antiquity, and is provided for in the " Sacramentaries," or
Prayer Books, of the early Church. The following
are some reasons why a custom so primitive and so
pious should be observed.

(1) The Holy Eucharist is essentially a sacrificial
act, offered up for the departed as well as The Eucharist
or the living. The petition in the Prayer an offering for
of Oblation, "humbly beseeching Thee to the departed
grant that by the merits and death of Thy Son Jesus
Christ and through faith in His blood, we and all Thy
whole Church may obtain remission of our sins and all
other benefits of His passion," is one which includes
the departed members of Christ's whole Church, or it
would be only a petition for a portion of the Church ;
and "all other benefits of His passion" seems especially to apply to the departed, as " remission of our

sins " applies to the living. " So that the virtue," says Bishop Cosin, " of this Sacrifice (which is here in this Prayer of Oblation commemorated and represented) doth not only extend itself to the living and those that are present, but likewise to them that are absent, and them that be already departed, or shall in time to come live and die in the faith of Christ." At no time could this benefit be so appropriately sought, as when for the last occasion the body of the deceased Christian lies in front of the Altar for association with Divine Service.

(2) A Funeral Eucharist is also an act of communion
an act of com- with the departed, by which we make an
munion with open recognition of our belief that he
them. still continues to be one of God's dear children ; that the soul in Paradise and the body in the grave are still the soul and body of one who is still a member of Christ, still a branch (as much as those who remain alive) of the true Vine.

(3) The Holy Communion being the special means
and a comfort by which the members of Christ are
to the mourners. brought near to their Divine Head, it is
to it that the surviving friends of the deceased may look for their chief comfort in bereavement. By it they may look to have their faith strengthened in Him who has proclaimed Himself to be " The Resurrection and the Life :" and by the strengthening of their faith they may hope to see, even in the burial of their loved ones, the promise of a better resurrection, when that which has borne the image of the earthly shall also bear the image of the Heavenly, when death shall be swallowed up in victory, and when God shall wipe away all tears from their eyes in the joy of a re-union before His Presence.

The Epistle and Gospel said at Funeral Communions are 1 Thess. iv. 13—18, and John vi. 37—40 : and Psalm xlii, " Like as the hart desireth the water brooks," is a most appropriate Introit.

§ 2. *The Service at the Grave.*

AFTER the Lesson, or after the Holy Communion, if it is celebrated, the funeral procession is again formed, " the Priest and Clerks " leading it from the Church to the Grave, and there singing or saying the ANTHEM, " Man that is born of a woman." The use of this soul-stirring Anthem is a noble peculiarity of the English Burial Service, though it was anciently used in the Church of England, and in some German Churches for a Compline Anthem on Saturday evenings.

The original composition of it is traced back to Notker, a monk of St. Gall, in Switzer- History of the land, at the close of the ninth century. It Anthem. is said to have been suggested by some such circumstances as those of the samphire gatherers on the cliff at Dover, which suggested a well-known passage in Shakspeare. As he watched men at some " dangerous trade," in which life hung on a thread, Notker sang, " In the midst of life we are in death," moulding his awful hymn to that familiar form of ancient days, " Holy God, Holy and Mighty, Holy and Immortal, have mercy upon us," which is found in the Primitive Liturgies. In the Middle Ages it was adopted as a Dirge on all melancholy occasions in Germany : armies used it as a battle song ; and superstitious ideas of its miraculous power rose to such a height, that, in the year 1316, the Synod of Cologne forbad the people to sing it at all, except on such occasions as

were allowed by their Bishop. A version of it by
Luther, " Mitten wir im Leben sind," is still very
popular in Germany, as a hymn.

When sung to such strains as befit its beautiful
Meaning of the words, this Anthem has a solemn magni-
Anthem.   ficence, and at the same time a wailing
prayerfulness, which makes it unsurpassable by any
similar portion of any ritual whatever.   It is the
prayer of the living for themselves and for the departed, when both are in the Presence of God for the
special object of a final separation (so far as this world
and visible things are concerned), until the great Day.
At such a season we do not argue about Prayers for
the departed, but we pray them.   For them and for
ourselves we plead the mercies of the Saviour before
the eternal Judge.   Not as selfish men, to whom the
brink of the grave brings thoughts of our own morta-
lity, do we tremblingly cry out for fear ; but as standing up before our dead who still live, as in anticipation
of the Day when we shall again stand together, dying
no more, before the Throne of the Judge, we acknowledge that Death is a mark of God's displeasure ; that
it is a result of sin, and that it ends in the bitter pains
of an eternal death, unless the holy, mighty, and merciful Saviour deliver us.   Such deep words of penitent
humiliation on our own behalf, and on that of the
person whose body is now to be removed from our
sight, are a fitting termination to the last hour which
is spent in the actual presence of those with whom we
have, perhaps, spent many hours which need the
mercy of God.

THE COMMENDATION of the deceased to the care
of Almighty God, in whose consecrated ground the
body is now laid, is a very ancient custom of the

Church; and in the Eastern Church it is accompanied by the striking words, "The earth is the Lord's, and the fulness thereof, the compass of the round world, and they that dwell therein," which well illustrates the meaning of the ceremony. The words used in our own Service are founded on several texts of Scripture: Eccles. xii. 7: Gen. xviii. 27: Gen. iii. 19: Phil. iii. 21. Their ancient form was free from the objection which is often made to them in the present day, beginning, ." I commend thy soul to God the Father Almighty, and thy body to the ground, earth to earth, ashes to ashes, dust to dust, in sure and certain hope of resurrection to eternal life through . . . ." In the Office for the Burial of the Dead at Sea another Form will be found, which has been substantially adopted by the American Church.

What the words really express, is this :—That (1) The body of a Christian, our "dear brother" in Christ (even if an erring brother), is being committed to the ground. That (2) God has taken him to Himself in the sense that his spirit has "returned to God who gave it." That (3) while we thus commit the body of one to the ground (who, whatever he was, was yet a sinner), we do it with faith in a future Resurrection of all. That (4) without any expression of judgment as to our departed brother, we will yet call that hope a "sure and certain hope," since it is founded on the Word of God.

Meaning of committal to the grave.

There may be cases in which persons have died in the actual committal of some grievous sin, and in which these words might be manifestly unsuitable ; but in such cases the whole Office is out of place, and the Clergyman should decline to use it. And in almost

I

all others, if not in all, there is room for an expression
of hope, in the spirit of charity in which the Church
appoints the words to be used ; and, as the Bishops
replied to the Puritans in 1661, " It is better to be
charitable and hope the best, than rashly to con-
demn."

THE LORD'S PRAYER is preceded by the " lesser
Litany," and by an ANTIPHON (formerly used as an
Antiphon to the Magnificat) taken from Rev. xiv. 13.
The sense thus given to the prayer of our Lord is that
of a thanksgiving for the rest which He has prepared
for the people of God in His Kingdom unseen.

Of the two beautiful prayers which follow, one is
called the COLLECT, and properly belongs to the celebration of the Holy Communion, where it takes the
place of the Collect for the day. Very little of the
wording of these two prayers is ancient; and their
noble language shows that there was a strongly vital
spirit of prayer in the Church of England at the time
of its Reformation, whose tone could well bear com-
parison with that of the ancient Church.

THE GRACE was added to the Office in 1661. The
"us all" is spoken with reference to the departed, as
well as ourselves.

[The following ancient Prayer is one which will
meet the wants of mourners who desire to pray for
their dear friends after their decease. Such Psalms as
the 42nd, 121st, and 130th are also appropriate for
private or family prayers.

" O God, whose nature and property is ever to have
mercy and to forgive, receive our humble petitions for the
soul of Thy servant whom Thou hast [this day] called to
depart out of this world : and because Thy servant hoped

and believed in Thee, we beseech Thee that Thou wilt neither suffer *him* to fall into the hand of the enemy, nor forget *him* for ever ; but wilt give Thine holy angels charge to receive *his* soul, and to transport it into the land of the living, there to be found worthy to rejoice in the fellowship of Thy saints ; through Jesus Christ our Lord, who ever liveth and reigneth with Thee in the Unity of the Holy Ghost, one God, world without end. *Amen.*"]

CHAPTER XII

The Churching of Women

" What reward shall I give unto the Lord for all the benefits that He hath done unto me?"—PSALM CXVI. 11.

THIS Service has been used in its present form[1] for many ages in the Church of England, and per-
History of the haps is the same that was referred to by
rite   , St. Gregory in a letter of advice that he wrote to St. Augustine, the first Archbishop of Canterbury, about the year of our Lord 601. It is, in fact, the Christian version of that ancient Jewish Service for the Purification of Women after Childbirth, which is ordained in the twelfth chapter of Leviticus ; and for which the Blessed Virgin Mary came up to Jerusalem (Luke ii. 22), to her " Churching" in the Temple.

This Christian custom of thanksgiving after childbirth is not, however, founded only on the Jewish custom, but on the first principles of religion. For the word of God to Eve was, " In sorrow thou shalt bring forth children." And as her first recorded words

[1] Except that Psalms 121 and 128 were used before the Reformation , the latter being also used in the Marriage Service.

after this sentence recognize the Providence of God in the matter of child-bearing, " I have gotten a man from the Lord," so the constant witness of religious parents has been, " Lo, children, and the fruit of the womb, are an heritage and gift that cometh of the Lord."

Thus two things make the association of a religious Service with child-bearing proper. First, Principles of the the fact that the giving or the withholding rite. of children is dependent on the Providence of God ; and, secondly, that the pain and sorrow which accompany it are a memorial of the transgression by which the mother of all living brought sin into the world. Every Christian mother is bound to acknowledge these facts by the act of worship which marks her return to the house of God.

Nor is this Service the only such acknowledgment required of a Christian mother by the Church.   The Rubric at the end of the Service says, " If there be a Communion, it is convenient that she receive the Holy Communion [2]."   For the Holy Communion carries up to God all other prayers and thanksgivings on the wings of sacrifice, and hence seals with a holy seal such a thanksgiving as this.   It also strengthens every act of prayer and every good resolution ; and hence is especially fitting for those who come to thank God for a recovery out of the depths of a weakness and sorrow mingled with " joy, that one is born into the world," that is sure to sober the heart, and make it dwell more than usual on the thoughts of God's goodness and the nearness of the unseen world.   Mothers should there-

[2] " Convenient " meant " fitting," or " right and proper," in the time when it was thus used in the Rubric.

fore make it a rule to receive the Holy Communion at
the same time that they are Churched, or (if there is
not a celebration on that day) as soon afterwards as is
possible.

There are two Psalms appointed in this Service, but
only one of them is to be used. The 116th is most
appropriate when the woman is going to communicate
after her Churching ; or where the death of the new-
born infant has been added to the sorrows of child-
bearing. The words, " You shall therefore give hearty
thanks unto God, *and say*," do not mean that the
woman is to repeat the Psalm or any other part of the
Service after the Priest ; but that the words to be used
are her words, spoken on her behalf. The Psalm
should be said by Priest and choir, as other Psalms
are said ; and so also should the responses.

It is undoubtedly intended that the Churching
Time and place Service should be said in the face of
for Churchings. the whole congregation ; and the most
proper time for it is immediately before Divine Service, especially the Holy Communion. The ancient
custom was, to say the Service near the Church door,
where the woman was kneeling, and then to lead her
by the hand into the Church (as a token of her return
to the house of God), with the words, " Enter thou
into the temple of God, that thou mayest have eternal
life, and live for ever." The choir-door seems a very
appropriate place for the ceremony; but the place is
left to custom and the discretion of the Clergyman.

The " offering" is a due to the Priest offered upon
the altar; but most Priests add it to the alms which
are offered at the Holy Communion for the poor, and
for other purposes connected with the Church.

No unmarried mother ought to be Churched, until

she has given evidence that she has truly repented of her sin. This evidence will be most effectually given by such a humble and contrite confession of it as will enable the Priest to minister God's Word of absolution after the example of our Lord, when, in a similar case, He said, " Go, and sin no more."

CHAPTER XIII

The Ordination Services

"And when they had ordained them elders in every church, and had prayed with fasting, they commended them to the Lord, on whom they believed."—ACTS xiv. 23.

THE Church of England retained at the Reformation, and still retains, the same general principles which it had previously held respecting the Ministry of the Church ; and the alterations made in the Ordination Offices were made chiefly with the purpose of condensing them, lessening the number of ceremonies, and bringing into greater prominence the central rite of Episcopal Imposition of Hands. Many alterations were made in the details of the Ordination Services between 1548 and 1661, but the substance of them is that which was used by the ancient Church.

These Services are three in number, the first being for the Ordering of Deacons; the second for the Ordering of Priests , and the third for the Consecration of Bishops. They are preceded by a PREFACE, supposed to have been written by Archbishop Cranmer ; and in this Preface the general principles are stated on which the Services are founded. The statements there made are as follows :—

1. There is evidence in Holy Scripture, and in the writings of ancient authors, that there have been Bishops, Priests, and Deacons in the Church of Christ from the time of the Apostles ; and this evidence is to be found by those who really study—"all men diligently reading "—the works in which it is contained.

2. None ever undertook these offices until (1) their qualifications for them had been proved to the satisfaction of lawful authority ; nor (2) until they had been properly ordained, with prayer and imposition of hands.

3. None shall be accounted a lawful Bishop, Priest, or Deacon in the Church of England, nor allowed to execute any of the functions belonging to those Orders, unless he has been ordained according to the forms of the Prayer Book.

4. Except when he has been previously consecrated or ordained by Bishops, or a Bishop, in some other Church.

5. Every man to be ordained Deacon must be twenty-three years of age ; every Deacon to be ordained Priest must be full twenty-four years of age ; and every Priest to be consecrated Bishop must be full thirty years of age.

6. Those to be ordained must be persons of good character, "learned in the Latin tongue, and sufficiently instructed in Holy Scripture."

7. Ordinations are to take place at the Ember Seasons, or else, upon some urgent occasion, upon some other Sunday or Holy Day, and in the face of the Church.

These general rules are in accordance with the ancient rules of the Church of England, and of the Catholic Church at large.

The actual Office for ordaining all three Orders, is made to form a portion of the Communion Service ; Deacons being ordained after the Epistle, Priests after the Gospel, and Bishops after the Nicene Creed. In each case, it is to be begun at some time after the ending of Morning Prayer ; and is preceded by the Litany, which is said as part of the office.

§ 1. *The Ordination of Deacons.*

BEFORE the Litany is said, at the Ordination of Deacons, a formal declaration as to their fitness for the office is made in the face of the Church by the Archdeacon, or by the person who has been made responsible for their due examination. Then the Bishop in person speaks to the congregation, and requires that if any persons know of any impediment for which the candidates should not be ordained Deacons, they are to come forth in the name of God, and declare it. A similar notice (called the "Si quis," from its first words, " If any") has been read in the Parish Church of each Candidate on some previous Sunday; so that every opportunity is given to the Laity of stating cases of notorious unfitness to the Bishop.

The LITANY is then sung or said, with a special clause, praying for those now to be made Deacons , and, after the Litany, the COMMUNION OFFICE is said with a Special Collect, Epistle, and Gospel ; the Deacons being ordained between the saying of the Epistle and the Gospel.

The Candidates are first required by the Bishop to answer several very solemn questions, their answers being given in a form which makes them equivalent to vows or oaths ; and hence the name of ORDINATION

Vows, as in the case of Baptismal Vows. The Bishop in one of these states what are the duties of the Deacon's office, which may be thus summed up :—(1) " To assist the Priest in Divine Service, and specially when he ministereth the Holy Communion ; and to help him in the distribution thereof." (2) To take part in the other Services of the Church. (3) To instruct the youth of the parish in the Catechism. (4) In the absence of the Priest, to baptize infants. (5) To take a subordinate share in the pastoral work of the parish. He is not qualified to pronounce Absolutions or Benedictions ; nor, of course, to celebrate the Holy Communion. He ought not, rightly, to take any part but that of *assisting* in Divine Service ; and it is very desirable, especially, that he should not perform the Marriage Service, but that a Priest should always be required for the purpose by the Laity.

As soon as these Vows have been taken, the Candidates kneel down before the Bishop to be changed from Laymen into Deacons. This is effected by the Bishop laying his hands separately on each of their heads, and saying these words :—

" Take thou authority to execute the office of a Deacon in the Church of God committed unto thee ; in the Name of the Father, and of the Son, and of the Holy Ghost. Amen."

A New Testament is then put into the hands of each as he is ordained, with the words :—

" Take thou authority to read the Gospel in the Church of God, and to preach the same, if thou be thereto licensed by the Bishop himself."

And when all are ordained, one of the new-made Deacons reads the Gospel of the day as a proclamation of the new office committed to him and the rest. The

Holy Communion is celebrated and administered; and, with another Special Collect before the Benediction, the Service concludes.

§ 2. *The Ordination of Priests.*

UP to the end of the Gospel, the Service for ordaining Priests is similar to that used for ordaining Deacons, a different Collect, Epistle, and Gospel being, however, appointed. After this, it is of a much more solemn character.

When the Gospel has been read, the Bishop reads an ADDRESS to the Deacons then to be ordained Priests, setting forth the responsibilities peculiar to the latter office ; and then follow the ORDINATION VOWS of Priests. They consist, substantially, of oaths that they will be faithful to the Church of England system in administering (1) the doctrine, (2) the Sacraments, and (3) the discipline of Christ : not drawing out their own ideas of what their duty is from the Scriptures, each one for himself, but ministering these "as the Lord hath commanded, and as *this Church and realm hath received the same*, according to the commandments of God." They also vow that they will enforce these " Church principles" upon others as far as lies in their power ; that they will " *teach the people* committed to their cure and charge with all diligence *to keep and observe the same."* In addition to this solemn promise that they will be faithful to the Church's principles and teach others to be so also, they vow they will do their best to put down what the Church considers to be error—they will "be ready, the Lord being their helper, with all faithful diligence, to banish and drive away all erroneous and strange doctrines contrary to God's

Word." The other Vows relate to the pastoral work of the Priest in admonishing those in sickness and those in health, and to his own personal life and conduct.

The Vows are confirmed by a beautiful BENEDIC-TION given by the Bishop, and then a short space or time is given for those present to offer their private prayers for the Candidates; after which the hymn VENI CREATOR, "Come, Holy Ghost, our souls inspire," is sung, as it has been sung here for many centuries in English Ordinations. This is succeeded by a prayer, in which the Bishop prays for God's Blessing on what he is going to do ; and then comes the act of Ordination.

This act consists, as with Deacons, in the Imposition of the Bishop's Hands upon the heads of the persons to be ordained. But in ordaining Priests, the Bishop does not act alone, some of the Clergy joining with him, and placing their hands with his on the heads of those who are thus to become their fellows. They do this as an act of assent, not as having the same power to give Orders which is possessed by the Bishop. The Bishop then says to each Candidate, as his hands and those of the assisting Priests rest on his head, the following awe-inspiring words :—

" Receive the Holy Ghost for the office and work or a Priest in the Church of God, now committed unto thee by the imposition of our hands. Whose sins thou dost forgive, they are forgiven ; and whose sins thou dost retain, they are retained. And be thou a faithful dispenser of the Word of God, and of His Holy Sacraments : in the Name of the Father, and of the Son, and of the Holy Ghost. Amen."

And he adds, delivering the Holy Bible to each one of them,—

" Take thou authority to preach the Word of God,

and to minister the Holy Sacraments in the congregation, where thou shalt be lawfully appointed thereunto."

The remaining portion of the Communion Office is then said ; and after all the newly ordained have communicated, a Special Collect and the Benediction close the Service.

The Priests thus ordained are now qualified (1) to offer sacrifice to God, viz., the Eucharistic Sacrifice, alms, oblations, and public prayers ; and (2) to administer grace to men, viz., the grace of the Sacraments, and all other ordinary supernatural gifts bestowed by God through His ministers.

§ 3. *The Consecration of Bishops*

THE Service for Consecrating Bishops begins with the Communion Office, which proceeds as far as the end of the Nicene Creed without any variation, except as to the Special Collect, Epistle, and Gospel. None but Bishops take part in it : and it is not until after the Nicene Creed that they say the Litany.

The Consecration part of the Service follows the Litany, and is very similar in its character to the Ordination of a Priest, the Vows made by the Bishop being, of course adapted to the higher spiritual position he is called to occupy. The essential part of the Service,—that which turns a Priest into a Bishop,—is the laying on of the hands of three or more Bishops upon the head of him who is to become by their act and word one of their own number, while the following solemn words are spoken by one of them :—

"Receive the Holy Ghost, for the office and work of

a Bishop in the Church of God, now committed unto thee by the imposition of our hands : In the Name of the Father, and of the Son, and of the Holy Ghost. Amen. And remember that thou stir up the grace of God which is given thee by this imposition of our hands : for God hath not given us the spirit of fear, but of power, and love, and soberness."

Then the Holy Bible is put into the new Bishop's hands, with an exhortation on the duties of the pastoral office as enjoined therein. Formerly the pastoral staff, which is carried before a Bishop on ceremonial occasions, was presented to him while the words, " Be to the flock of Christ a shepherd, and not a wolf," were being spoken ; and a ring was placed on his finger, to signify his entire devotion to Christ and the Church, as if he were even wedded thereto. But these usages have been discontinued in recent times.

The Service concludes, as in the other cases, with the celebration and administration of the Holy Communion, a Special Collect being said before the Benediction.

A Bishop has spiritual ability to do all that he could previously do as a Priest ; and also further (1), to continue the succession of the ministry by ordaining Bishops, Priests, and Deacons, and (2) to perfect the Christian condition of the Baptized by Confirmation. In addition to this, he is also the chief pastor and head of his diocese, both as regards the Laity and the Clergy. He is empowered to direct and to govern them in all spiritual concerns, and stands nearest to his Divine Master of all that Master's earthly servants. For his responsible office he receives an additional gift of the Holy Spirit's power ; and if, in devout reliance on his Master, he " stirs up the gift " that is bestowed on him, a spiritual wisdom will be the result, such as cannot be looked for in the inferior orders of the Ministry. An assembly of Bishops solemnly gathered together with prayer for the guidance of the Holy Spirit, is thus the highest spiritual authority on earth to which the Church can appeal for guidance.

In respect to all the orders of the Ministry, faithful Laymen will often carry out the Apostolic injunction, "Brethren, pray for us." And on the Ember Days, especially, they will remember how great an interest they have in the work of Ordination, and beseech Almighty God that He will give His grace to the Clergy, that they may faithfully serve before Him to the glory of His great Name, and the benefit of His Holy Church.

CHAPTER XIV

𝔉𝔢𝔰𝔱𝔦𝔟𝔞𝔩𝔰

"Some of them hath He made High Days, and hallowed them."—ECCLUS. xxxiii. 9.

THE principal events of our Blessed Lord's life at once stamped themselves upon the memory of His disciples in so indelible a manner, that, as the days came round on which they occurred, the religious celebration of the day by special acts of Divine Worship became a matter of course. Thus the first day of each week commemorated His Resurrection, and the sixth day His Death ; and the anniversaries of those events were days of strictest mourning or of highest joy.

Origin of Christian Feasts.

From the observance of these days in memory of our Lord, sprang that of others, commemorating those persons most nearly associated with Him in His work and holiness ; and eventually the martyrs who died for His Name's sake, and whose memory was reverenced by their brethren.

Thus arose the Festival system of the Church, in which particular days are distinguished as "high days," and "hallowed" more or less by additional religious observances.

K

§ 1. *Festivals of the Church of England.*

WHEN the devotional system of the Church of England was re-formed, it was thought expedient to diminish the number of Festivals, some having been set apart in memory of persons whose existence was doubtful, and others in memory of those who had no particular claim to be classed among Saints, not being conspicuous for great holiness or great works of love. The number of Festivals was thus reduced to 149, including Sundays, which may be classified as follows :—

In honour of our Blessed Lord (including 50 Lord's Days)	63
————— God the Holy Ghost	3
————— the Holy Trinity	1
————— the Holy Angels	1
————— the Blessed Virgin Mary	5
————— St. John Baptist, the Apostles, and others associated with our Lord .	22
————— other Saints	54
	149

Of these Festivals, 82, including Sundays, are marked by " Proper " Prefaces, Collects, Epistles, Gospels, Psalms and Lessons ; some or all of these specialities distinguishing them from days of ordinary Divine Service ; while others are only noted in the Calendar which is printed at the beginning of the Prayer Book. They are also distinguished from ordinary days by Proper Hymns, and by changes in the colour of the Altar Coverings and the Sacerdotal Vestments . but these latter observances form part of an exact attention to the proprieties of Church customs, which is not at present universal in the Church of England.

§ 2. *Festivals in Honour of our Lord.*

Sundays.	
Christmas Day	Dec. 25
The Circumcision	Jan. 1.
— Epiphany	— 6.
Easter Day . . . . ⎱	
—— Monday and Tuesday . . . . ⎰	moveable.
Ascension Day . . . . ⎰	
*Invention of the Cross	May 3.
*Lammas Day	Aug. 1.
*The Transfiguration	— 6
*Name of Jesus	— 7.
*Holy Cross Day	Sept. 14
*O Sapientia	Dec. 16.

SUNDAY has been universally observed by Christians since our Lord's Resurrection upon "the first day of the week." By that Resurrection our Lord consecrated it for ever as "The Lord's Day." He made it the special Day on which to vouchsafe His visible Presence to the Apostles and Disciples between His Resurrection and Ascension ; and the coming of the Holy Ghost on the Day of Pentecost still further dedicated it to most sacred memories.

The principles of its observance are founded on the fact indicated by the name. It is the *Lord's* Day, not our own ; the day dedi- {How to keep Sunday.} cated to the Sun of Righteousness, of which the first object is that it should be used for His worship. It is

* Minor Festivals, or "Black Letter" days.

also a day of rest, not for man only, but ordinarily for all that is subject to man—a day when no hard service or labour, for man's advantage, should be exacted of any living thing, and none but necessary work done. Divine worship, religious meditation and reading, with a cheerful and thankful repose, which is not idleness, are the proper objects which most persons should set before themselves on the Lord's Day; while active works of love are required from a few, and some necessary employments of all

The Prayer Book provides for the celebration of the Holy Eucharist on every Lord's Day; and its omission from the Services of the day is a grave departure from the spirit of Christianity, as well as from the rule of the Church.

CHRISTMAS DAY is the day when God makes us glad with the yearly remembrance of the birth of His only Son Jesus Christ our Lord. It is most fit that the season marked out by angels with songs of joy, such as had not been heard on earth since the Creation, should also be observed as a time of festive gladness by the Church and in the social life of Christians. Christ Himself instituted the festival for us when He sanctified the day by then first bringing His human nature into sight. The holy angels witnessed to its separation for ever as a day of days, when they proclaimed the Glory that was then offered to God in the highest by the salvation of man, and the peace that was brought among men on earth through their reconciliation to God. Even beyond the Church the Christmas gladness of the Church spreads itself abroad among men; and a common Christian instinct teaches all to regard it as a season of unity, fellowship, good-will, happiness, and peace.

The festival of Christmas is extended through the week by the festivals of St. Stephen, St. John the Evangelist, and the Holy Innocents ; and the direction for the Proper Preface in the Communion Service to be read "upon Christmas Day and seven days after," shows that the whole octave (or eight days) is to be considered as part of the festival.

THE CIRCUMCISION is in fact the octave day of Christmas, which has the incident of that day added to the Commemoration of Christmas to do the more honour to the festival of our Lord's Nativity. Its observance as New Year's Day ought not to eclipse its religious observance as a Church festival in honour of our Divine Redeemer[1].

THE EPIPHANY commemorates the revelation of our Lord's Divine Glory to the Gentiles, as represented by the three Wise Men from the East. The Scriptures used on this day beautifully illustrate its object : " Arise, shine , for thy Light is come, and the glory of the Lord is risen upon thee . . . . And the Gentiles shall come to thy Light, and kings to the brightness of Thy rising." A memorial of the offerings made by the wise men is still retained in a custom of our English Sovereigns, who make an oblation of gold, frankincense, and myrrh at the altar of the Chapel Royal on this festival, either in person or by an officer of the household appointed to represent them.

. By the festival and season of Epiphany, the Church acknowledges the Holy Child to be her God ; and adores the Light of the World arising to shine upon her from the manger-cradle at Bethlehem.

---

[1] The year began on March 25th until 1752, when an Act of Parliament changed New Year's Day to January 1st.

EASTER DAY.—They who went about "preaching Jesus and the Resurrection," must have remembered with joyous devotion every anniversary of their
Lord's restoration to them. A trace of their joy is still
retained in the Eastern Church, where friends salute
each other on Easter morning with the words, "The
Lord is risen." Formerly, there was a procession in
our churches before Divine Service on this day, with
anthems ; but these are now used before the Proper
Psalms, instead of the Venite.

The name of the festival has, doubtless, been derived
from the idea of sun-rising, the natural rising of the
sun being taken as a type of the rising of the Sun of
Righteousness from the darkness of the grave. A
similar feeling towards the East has led Christians to
build their churches looking in that direction, to worship towards the East, and to be laid in the grave as
those who wish to rise with their faces towards the
Sunrise of the Resurrection

Easter is extended through the week, like Christmas,
by the Monday and Tuesday festivals , and the following Sunday ("Low Sunday") closes the octave. Easter
Day itself must occur on some day between March 22
and April 25, or on one of those days.

ASCENSION DAY, or Holy Thursday (the 40th
day after Easter Day), is one of the principal festivals,
like Christmas and Easter, and has an octave as they
have. For, as our Lord consecrated Christmas Day
by being born, and Easter by rising from the dead, so
He hallowed Ascension Day by carrying our human
nature from earth and hell to heaven, and thus com-
pleting His triumph over evil. The festival concludes
the yearly commemoration of the great acts of our
Lord's life and work ; which thus leads upwards from

the cradle at Bethlehem, exhibiting before God and man the various stages of His redeeming work, and following Him, step by step, until we stand with the disciples gazing up after Him, as He goes within the everlasting doors. There is no reason whatever why it should not be observed with the same solemnity as Christmas Day, the first of the series.

The "minor festivals" associated with our Lord are not days of the same solemnity, and have not any special Services appointed for them. THE INVENTION OF THE CROSS is a perpetual memorial of the finding of our Lord's Cross by the Empress Helena, about A.D. 326. LAMMAS DAY has come down to us from Saxon times; and is thought by some to have been instituted as a day of thanksgiving, when the first-fruits of the corn were offered on the altar. Others consider that the name is not *Hlaf-mæsse*, or Loaf-mass, but Lamb-mass. The object of the festival is involved in obscurity, but we may reverently associate it with the " Corn of Wheat," whose dying produced the harvest that fills the heavenly garner, and with the Lamb of God which taketh away the sins of the world. THE TRANSFIGURATION commemorates the mystery indicated by its name, and has been in the Calendar for about 1400 years; but it was never observed as a principal festival of our Lord. THE NAME OF JESUS is a memorial of that Holy Name at which every knee should bow, and in which countless miracles have been wrought. HOLY CROSS DAY was instituted as a memorial of the day on which the Empress Helena caused a portion of Christ's Cross to be set up in the great church which she had built at Jerusalem. It also commemorates the appearance of the " Sign of the Son of Man" in the heavens to Constantine, which

was the great means of converting him, and so making
Christianity the established religion of the Roman
Empire. O SAPIENTIA, are words that mark the
first of six days on which the glory of Christ's Advent
was commemorated by anthems which began with
some of the titles given Him in prophecy. This one
was, " O Wisdom, which cometh forth from the Most
High, reaching from the one end of all things to
the other, mighty and sweetly ordering all things ;
come, that thou mayest teach us the way of understanding."

§ 3. *Festivals in honour of the Holy Ghost and the
Blessed Trinity.*

WHITSUN DAY, or *Pentecost* (the seventh Sunday
after Easter Day), commemorates the descent of the
Holy Ghost upon the Apostles, to abide with the
Church for ever, according to the promise of our Lord ;
and it has been observed from the very beginning.
The Jewish festival of Pentecost is supposed to have
been instituted by God as a memorial of the day on
which He gave the Law to Moses, and declared the
Israelites " a peculiar treasure, a kingdom of Priests,
and an holy nation " (Exod. xix. 5, 6) an object of the
day which makes its connexion with Whitsun Day, the
day when the Holy Ghost descended to sanctify a new
Israel for " a peculiar people and a royal Priesthood,"
very significant. But the prominent character of the
day was that of a solemn harvest festival. Fifty days
previously, the first-cut sheaf of *corn* was offered to
God for a blessing on the harvest then about to begin.
On the Day of Pentecost two loaves of the first new
bread were offered (with appointed burnt-offerings) in

thanksgiving for the harvest then ended ; and this aspect of the feast has also a striking significance. For, as Christ was the "Corn of Wheat" which (having "fallen into the ground and died" on the day of the Passover) had borne much fruit when It sprung up a new and perpetual Sacrifice to God on Easter Day, so the 5000 baptized on the day of Pentecost were the first offering to God of the "One Bread" of the Lord's Body (1 Cor. x. 17). The festival is extended through the week by Whitsun Monday and Whitsun Tuesday; but its octave day is a great festival of itself, viz. :—

TRINITY SUNDAY.—This day (the eighth Sunday after Easter Day) commemorates the consummation of God's saving work, and the perfect revelation to the Church of the Three Persons in One God as the sole objects of worship. The love of each Person is commemorated in the separate holy days which memorialize before God and man the Incarnation, Death, Resurrection, and Ascension of our Lord ; and the sending forth of the Spirit by the Father and the Son, on Whitsun Day. In the festival of Trinity all these solemn subjects of belief are gathered into one act of worship, as the Church Militant looks upward through the door opened in heaven, and bows down in adoration with the Church Triumphant, saying, "Holy, holy, holy, Lord God Almighty, which was, and is, and is to come .... Thou art worthy, O Lord, to receive glory, and honour, and power ; for Thou hast created all things, and for Thy pleasure they are and were created."

§ 4. *Festival in honour of the Holy Angels.*

MICHAELMAS DAY is a memorial of the communion between the redeemed children of God and the holy Angels "Ye are come unto Mount Sion, and unto the city of the living God, the heavenly Jerusalem, and to an innumerable company of angels." to the company of those who sang anthems of joy at the birth of Jesus, who comforted Him in His agony, and who, on many occasions, have shown that they are "ministering spirits, sent forth to minister for them who shall be heirs of salvation." This association of these unfallen beings with fallen but redeemed man, is a fact which the festival of St. Michael and all Angels commemorates yearly before God and man; and every time the Holy Eucharist is celebrated, in the Preface to the Sanctus, which is, "Therefore with angels and archangels, and all the company of Heaven, we laud and magnify Thy glorious Name, evermore praising Thee, and saying Holy, Holy, Lord God of hosts, heaven and earth are full of Thy glory: Glory be to Thee, O Lord most High." The Scriptures of the day very fully illustrate this festival.

§ 5. *Festivals in honour of the Blessed Virgin Mary.*

The Purification	Feb. 2.
— Annunciation	March 25.
* — Visitation	July 2
* — Nativity	Sept. 8.
* — Conception	Dec. 8.

The first two of these days have Special Services appointed: the other three are included among the minor holy days.

THE PURIFICATION. This festival has a double

* Minor Festivals, or "Black Letter" days.

title, which is, in full, " *The Presentation of Christ in the Temple, commonly called The Purification of St. Mary the Virgin."* This connexion of the two events is, doubtless, to show the close relation which the acts of the Blessed Virgin bore to the Incarnation of our Lord ; and that she is most honoured by associating her with her Divine Son. The common name of this festival is *Candlemas Day,* from a very ancient ceremony of walking in procession with lighted candles, and singing hymns. It is the fortieth day after Christmas, that being the period at which the rites of Churching and Presentation were enjoined by the Law, to which our Lord thus showed His obedience, and the Blessed Virgin her humility. As the one had no original sin, so the other needed no ceremonial purification after His holy conception and birth. But, as at Christ's Baptism, so at His Presentation in the Temple, He says, " Suffer it to be so now, for thus it becometh us to fulfil all righteousness."

THE ANNUNCIATION, a very ancient festival of the Church, called in the Calendar of Proper Lessons " *the Annunciation of our Lady,"* and commonly, " *Lady Day."* Being the 25th of March, it is exactly nine months before Christmas Day, and thus marks the fact of our Lord's Incarnation at the very time when the words of the angel were fulfilled by the Holy Ghost overshadowing the Blessed Virgin. On this day the year began under the " Old Style."

The other three days commemorate THE VISITATION of Mary to her cousin Elizabeth, her CONCEPTION, and her NATIVITY, and do not call for any remark.

The holiness of the Blessed Virgin, through her association with her Divine Son, has always been kept vividly in view by the Church; but while excess of sentiment has led to the dishonour of her name by speaking of her as if she herself were Divine, so want of faith in the principle of the Incarnation has led to an irreverent depreciation of her holiness. Our two principal and three minor festivals show the true course to follow : to esteem her above all other Saints as the Mother of our Lord, but yet to honour her so that her honour may be to the glory of God.

§ 6. *Festivals in honour of Saints associated with our Lord.*

Conversion of St. Paul the Apostle . . .	Jan. 25
St. Matthias the Apostle	Feb. 24.
St Mark the Evangelist	April 25
St. Philip and St James the Apostles . .	May 1.
*St. John the Evangelist, before the Latin Gate	— 6.
St. Barnabas the Apostle	June 11.
Nativity of St. John the Baptist . . .	— 24
St. Peter the Apostle	— 29.
*St Mary Magdalen	July 22.
St. James the Apostle	— 25.
*St. Anne, mother of the Blessed Virgin . .	— 26.
St Bartholomew the Apostle	Aug. 24.
*Beheading of St. John the Baptist	— 29.
St. Matthew the Apostle	Sept. 21.
St Luke the Evangelist	Oct. 18.
St Simon and St Jude the Apostles . . .	— 28.
All Saints	Nov. 1.
St Andrew the Apostle	— 30.
St. Thomas the Apostle	Dec. 21.
St. Stephen, the first Martyr	— 26.
St John the Evangelist	— 27.
The Holy Innocents	— 28.

* Minor Festivals, or " Black Letter" days.

§ 7. *Minor Festivals in honour of other Saints, with the dates of their deaths.*

DIED.	MARTYRS IN THE GREAT PERSECUTIONS.	FESTIVAL.
A. D.		
90	St. Nicomede, Roman priest . . .	June 1.
100	St. Clement, Bishop of Rome . . .	Nov. 23
203	St. Perpetua, African lady	Mar. 7.
230	St. Cecilia, Roman lady	Nov. 22.
250	St. Fabian, Bishop of Rome . . .	Jan. 20.
251	St. Agatha, Sicilian lady	Feb. 5.
258	St. Lawrence, Archdeacon of Rome .	Aug. 10.
258	St. Cyprian, Bishop of Carthage . .	Sept. 26.
270	St. Valentine, Bishop or Priest . .	Feb. 14.
272	St. Denys, Archbishop of Paris . .	Oct. 9.
275	St. Prisca, young Roman lady . . .	Jan. 18.
278	St. Margaret, of Antioch	July 20.
290	St. Lucian, French Priest	Jan. 8.
290	St. Faith, young French lady . . .	Oct. 6.
304	St. Agnes, young Roman lady . . .	Jan. 21.
304	St. Vincent, Spanish Deacon . . .	— 22.
305	St. Lucy, young lady of Syracuse . .	Dec. 13.
307	St. Catharine, princess	Nov. 25.
308	St. Crispin, Roman Missionary . .	Oct. 25.
316	St. Blasius, Armenian Bishop . . .	Feb. 3.
	MARTYRS AND OTHER SAINTS SPE- CIALLY CONNECTED WITH ENG- LAND.	
290	St. George, Roman officer, Martyr .	April 23.
303	St. Alban, English officer, Martyr .	June 17.
326	St. Nicolas, Bishop of Myra . . .	Dec. 6.
543	St. Benedict, Italian Abbot . . .	Mar. 21.
544	St. David, Welsh Archbishop . . .	— 1.
560	St. Machutus, Welsh Bishop of St. Malo	Nov. 15.
604	St. Gregory, Bishop of Rome . . .	Mar. 12.
604	St. Augustine, Archbishop of Canter- bury	May 26.

DIED.	MARTYRS AND OTHER SAINTS SPE-CIALLY CONNECTED WITH ENG-LAND.—(*Continued.*)	FESTIVAL.
A.D		
670	St Etheldreda, English Queen . .	Oct. 17.
673	St. Chad, Bishop of Lichfield . . .	Mar 2.
725	St Giles, French Abbot	Sept. 1
735	Venerable Bede, Monk of Jarrow .	May 27.
755	St. Boniface, English Archbishop of Mentz	June 5
862	St Swithin, Bishop of Winchester .	July 15
870	St Edmund, English King and Martyr	Nov 20.
978	St Edward, English King ⎱ death . .	Mar. 18.
	and Martyr . . ⎰ translation	June 20
988	St. Dunstan, Archbishop of Canterbury	May 19.
1012	St. Alphege, Archbishop of Canterbury	April 19.
1066	St. Edward, King and Confessor . .	Oct. 13.
1200	St. Hugh, Bishop of Lincoln . . .	Nov 17
1253	St. Richard, Bishop of Chichester .	April 3.
	FRENCH AND OTHER SAINTS	
335	St. Silvester, Bishop of Rome . . .	Dec. 31
340	St Enurchus, Bishop of Orleans .	Sept. 7.
368	St. Hilary, Bishop of Poictiers, Confessor	Jan 13
397	St. Ambrose, Bishop of Milan .	April 4.
397	St Martin, Bishop of Tours . . .	July 4
420	St. Jerome, Italian Priest	Sept. 30.
430	St Augustine, Bishop of Hippo . .	Aug 28.
444	St. Britius, Bishop of Tours . .	Nov. 13
535	St Remigius, Bishop of Rheims . .	Oct. 1.
559	St. Leonard, Confessor . .	Nov. 6
709	St Lambert, Bishop of Maestricht .	Sept. 17.

Some of these are the names of saints to whom the Church is only less indebted than to the Holy Apostles themselves; and it is to be regretted that those of others, such as St. Aidan, St. Cuthbert, St. Thomas of Canterbury, and the great Eastern saints have been omitted.

CHAPTER XV

ℱasts

*" Sanctify ye a fast, call a solemn assembly, gather the elders
and all the inhabitants of the land into the house of the
Lord your God."*—JOEL i. 14.

AS the Festivals of the Church originated in the joy
of Easter, so the Fasts originated Origin of
in the sorrow of Good Friday. Christian Fasts.

The institution of fasting, and the observance of
Fast Days was, indeed, handed down to the Christian
Church from the Old Dispensation our Lord adopted
while He lived on earth ; and He told His disciples
that they should fast (as they afterwards did) when the
Bridegroom should be taken away from them. In the
Primitive Church many Fast Days were observed, and
with great strictness. " There are those," wrote St.
Chrysostom (A.D. 347—407) " who rival Primitive modes
one another in fasting, and show a mar- of fasting.
vellous emulation in it. Some, indeed, who spend two
whole days without food ; and others who reject
from their tables the use of wine, oil, and every deli-
cacy, and, taking only bread and water, persevere in
this practice during the whole of Lent." Many such
testimonies to the habits of the early Church of Christ

show that the later habits of the Church are such as the Apostles are likely to have originated ; and that a Church without Fasts would be very unlike that which they established. The Church of England, therefore, continued the observance of them at the Reformation, set forth two instructive Homilies on the subject of fasting, and inserted in the Prayer Book a list of the days to be kept. This list comprises the following days :—

1. All Fridays.
2. The week-days of Lent.
3. The Ember days.
4. The Rogation days.
5. The Evens or Vigils.

§ 1. *Fridays.*

THE Sundays being memorial days of our Lord's Resurrection, the Fridays are, likewise, memorial days of His Death ; and have been so observed from the earliest ages of Christianity. And as Easter Day is the crown of all Sundays, so Good Friday is the Great Friday of the year, the type of all the others. Ordinary Fridays are marked in the public Services of the Church by the use of the Litany, the penitential sense of which ought to be kept prominently in view then ; and if hymns are used at Morning and Evening Prayer, they are usually selected with reference to the Cross and Passion of our Lord, and the sin of mankind, for which He suffered. But the Friday should Mode of   also be distinguished from other days of keeping Friday. the week in the private life of Christians, by abstinence from animal food, or, where that is not expedient, from delicacies. Such an observance of the

Fridays of our weeks gives a more festive character to our Sundays—"sets them off," as we say—and is a great help towards the proper discipline of the soul.

GOOD FRIDAY should be observed with greater strictness than any other ; and its solemn observance ought to be considered as very binding. No work should be done but what is of the most necessary kind : a reverent silence (at least, to the extent of abstinence from trivial conversation) should be kept : Divine Service should be attended : and only as much of the plainest food taken as is necessary to prevent illness[1]. Opinions are much divided as to the propriety of celebrating and receiving the Holy Communion on Good Friday. Until the Reformation, it was customary to reserve some portion of what had been consecrated on Maundy Thursday. But as nothing is said about such reservation in the Prayer Book, it is to be concluded that the Collects, Epistle, and Gospel were intended to be used at a Celebration, as on all other occasions when these are appointed.

The purpose of observing Good Friday is (1) to memorialize God of the Passion of our Lord Jesus Christ ; and (2) to discipline the soul by the remembrance of the same Passion. And as each Sunday is, in its degree, an Easter, so each Friday is a lesser memorial day of the Cross of Christ.

§ 2. *Lent.*

THE forty days' fast before Easter, is an institution which has come down to us from the History of Primitive Church. In some countries the Lent.

---

[1] The Cross-bun represents this small quantity of plain and necessary food.

forty days were extended over eight or nine weeks, instead of six, by the omission of Sundays, Thursdays, and Saturdays, or Sundays and Saturdays, from the number of fasting days—thus beginning it at Sexagesima or Septuagesima. But for many ages the practice of the Church has been to omit Sundays only, and so to extend Lent during the six weeks from Ash Wednesday to Easter Eve, including both days.

The first object of the institution of Lent was doubt-

Meaning and purpose of Lent. less that of perpetuating in the hearts of every generation of Christians the sorrow and mourning which the Apostles and other Disciples felt during the time that the Bridegroom was taken away from them. This sorrow had, indeed, been turned into joy by the Resurrection ; yet no Easter joys could ever erase from the mind of the Church the memory of those awful forty hours of blank and desolation which followed the last sufferings of our Lord ; and she lives over year by year the time from the morning of Good Friday to the morning of Easter Day by a re-presentation of Christ evidently set forth, crucified among us. This probably was the earliest idea of a fast before Easter. But it almost necessarily followed that sorrow concerning the death of Christ should be accompanied by sorrow concerning the cause of that death ; and hence the Lenten fast became a season of spiritual discipline, and was so, probably, from Apostolic times. According also to the literal habit which the early Church had of looking up to the pattern set by our Divine Master, the forty days of His fasting in the wilderness, while He was undergoing temptation, became the rule of His servants' Lent, deriving still more force, as an example from the typical prophecy of it which is evident in the case of Moses and Elijah.

It is difficult to lay down rules respecting fasting that will be at all generally applicable. Mode of fasting The objects of it are well stated, however, in present day. in the first Homily on the subject. (1) "To chastise the flesh, that it be not too wanton, but tamed and brought in subjection to the spirit." (2) "That the spirit may be more fervent and earnest in prayer." (3) "That our fast be a testimony and witness with us before God, of our humble submission to His high Majesty."

Keeping these three objects in view, common sense and a real desire to make abstinence from food and luxuries answer a spiritual end, will lead any rational person to a judicious and pious rule of fasting applicable to their own case.

Most persons may diminish the quantity of their food on fast days without any harm resulting; many can even *abstain safely from animal food* altogether. All can deny themselves such delicacies as they may properly enjoy on other days, and can also abstain from mere amusements.

§ 3. *The Ember Days.*

THERE are four special Sundays appointed for Ordinations, and three days in each preceding week are to be observed as Days of Abstinence. These three days are called Ember Days, either from the old Saxon word "Ymbren," to run a round, or from the Latin title, "Quatuor Tempora," corrupted into Quatember in German, and Ember in English.

The Ordination Sundays are the Second Sunday in

Lent, Trinity Sunday, the Sunday after Holy Cross
Day, and the Sunday after St. Lucy's Day ; so that the
Ember days are .—

The *Wednesday, Friday,*
and *Saturday* after
{
The First Sunday in Lent,
Whitsun Day,
September 14th,
December 13th.
}

A special Collect is appointed (one of two among
the Occasional Prayers) to be used at Morning and
Evening Prayer on the Ember Days; and it is a continual witness before God and man of the interest
which the whole body of the Church has in the ordination of the Clergy who are to minister in it.   The
entreaty of St. Paul, "Brethren, pray for us," continually goes forth to the Church at large from the
Clergy ; but never with greater necessity, or with
greater force, than when the solemn act of Ordination
is about to be performed by the Bishops, and a number of the future guides and pastors of the Church are
about to be empowered and authorized to undertake
their office.   Not only the Clergy, therefore, but the
Laity also, should keep these days in mind, and pray
for God's blessing on the ministry of the Church.

§ 4. *The Rogation Days.*

THE *Monday, Tuesday,* and *Wednesday* before
Ascension Day are called by the name of Rogation
Days, from the Latin word *rogare*, to ask, or pray.
They are days on which to ask the blessing of God on
the fruits of the earth, and were formerly, as still in
some places, celebrated by processions with prayer
around the boundaries of the parish.   There is a
Homily for special use on these days, showing the
importance that was formerly attached to them ; and

the Litany should be used on each day. It is very desirable that a religious character should be given to the " Beating of Bounds ;" and this may be done by singing the 103rd Psalm at each halting-place, and offering up for a prayer the clause of the Litany, " That it may please Thee to give and preserve to our use the kindly fruits of the earth, so as in due time we may enjoy them : We beseech thee to hear us, good Lord."

§ 5. *The Evens or Vigils.*

ALL festivals, including Sundays, are preceded by Eves, which are a religious anticipation of the days themselves. Some have also Vigils, which are fast days until Evensong. Some festivals have, however, no Vigil appointed, because they occur during seasons which are otherwise festive, or are preceded by one of the minor festivals or " Black Letter Days." The following is the Prayer Book list of the VIGILS or EVENS :—

" The Evens or Vigils before
- The Nativity of our Lord.
- The Purification of the Blessed Virgin *Mary.*
- The Annunciation of the Blessed Virgin.
- Easter Day.
- Ascension Day.
- Pentecost.
- *St. Matthias.*
- *St. John Baptist.*
- *St. Peter.*
- *St. James.*
- *St. Bartholomew.*
- *St. Matthew.*
- *St. Simon* and *St. Jude.*
- *St. Andrew.*
- *St. Thomas.*
- All Saints.

NOTE,—That if any of these Feast-Days fall upon a *Monday*, then the Vigil or Fast-Day shall be kept upon the *Saturday*, and not upon the *Sunday* next before it."

Index.

THE END.

New Works

IN COURSE OF PUBLICATION BY

Messrs. RIVINGTON,

WATERLOO PLACE, LONDON;

HIGH STREET, OXFORD   TRINITY STREET, CAMBRIDGE.

SEPTEMBER, 1871.

DICTIONARY OF DOCTRINAL AND HISTORICAL THEOLOGY.
By VARIOUS WRITERS.

Edited by the Rev. John Henry Blunt, M.A., F.S.A., Editor of 'The Annotated Book of Common Prayer.'

One vol., imperial 8vo. 42s.

The Principles of the CATHEDRAL SYSTEM
VINDICATED and FORCED upon MEMBERS of CATHEDRAL FOUNDATIONS.

Eight Sermons, preached in the Cathedral Church of the Holy and Undivided Trinity of Norwich.

By Edward Meyrick Goulburn, D.D., Dean of Norwich, late Prebendary of St. Paul's, and one of Her Majesty's Chaplains.

Crown 8vo. 5s.

LONDON, OXFORD, & CAMBRIDGE.

ELEMENTS OF RELIGION.

Lectures delivered at St. James's, Piccadilly, in Lent, 1870.
By **Henry Parry Liddon**, D.D , D.C.L., Canon of St. Paul's, and
Ireland Professor of Exegesis in the University of Oxford.

Crown 8vo.   *[In the Press.*

A MANUAL OF LOGIC;

Or, a Statement and Explanation of the Laws of Formal Thought.
By **Henry J. Turrell**, M.A., Oxon.

Square crown 8vo.   2s. 6d.

THE PSALMS translated from the HEBREW.

With Notes, chiefly Exegetical.
By **William Kay**, D D., Rector of Great Leighs; late Principal of
Bishop's College, Calcutta.

8vo.   12s. 6d.

SERMONS.

By **Henry Melvill**, B.D., late Canon of St. Paul's, and Chaplain
in Ordinary to the Queen.

New Edition.   Two vols.   Crown 8vo.   5s. each.

THE ORIGIN AND DEVELOPMENT OF RELIGIOUS BELIEF.

By **S. Baring-Gould**, M A., Author of 'Curious Myths of the
Middle Ages.'

PART I. MONOTHEISM AND POLYTHEISM. *8vo.   15s.*
PART II. CHRISTIANITY. *8vo.   15s.*

PARISH MUSINGS; or, DEVOTIONAL POEMS.

By **John S. B. Monsell**, LL D , Rural Dean, and Rector of
St. Nicholas Guildford.

New Edition.   Small 8vo.   5s.
Also a Cheap Edition.   18mo.   Limp cloth, 1s. 6d.; or in cover, 1s.

LONDON, OXFORD, & CAMBRIDGE.

THE WITNESS of ST. JOHN to CHRIST;

Being the Boyle Lectures for 1870.

With an Appendix on the Authorship and Integrity of St. John's Gospel and the Unity of the Johannine Writings.

By the Rev. **Stanley Leathes**, M.A., Minister of St. Philip's, Regent Street, and Professor of Hebrew, King's College, London.

8vo. 10*s.* 6*d.*

THE ELEGIES OF PROPERTIUS,

Translated into English Verse.

By **Charles Robert Moore**, M.A., late Scholar of Corpus Christi College, Oxford.

Small 8vo. 2*s.* 6*d.*

'THE ATHANASIAN CREED,'

And its Usage in the English Church: an Investigation as to the Original Object of the Creed and the Growth of prevailing Misconceptions regarding it.

A Letter to the Very Reverend W. F. Hook, D.D., F.R.S., Dean of Chichester, from **C. A. Swainson**, D.D., Canon of the Cathedral, and Examining Chaplain to the Lord Bishop of Chichester; Norrisian Professor of Divinity, Cambridge.

Crown 8vo. 3*s.* 6*d.*

PRAYERS AND MEDITATIONS FOR THE HOLY COMMUNION.

With a Preface by **C. J. Ellicott**, D.D., Lord Bishop of Gloucester and Bristol.

With Rubrics in red. *Royal 32mo.* 2*s.* 6*d.*

THE SHEPHERD OF HERMAS.

Translated into English, with an Introduction and Notes.

By **Charles H. Hoole**, M.A., Senior Student of Christ Church, Oxford.

Fcap. 8vo. 4*s.* 6*d.*

MATERIALS AND MODELS FOR GREEK AND LATIN PROSE COMPOSITION.

Selected and Arranged by J. Y. Sargent, M.A. Tutor, late Fellow of Magdalen College, Oxford; and T. F. Dallin, M.A., Fellow and Tutor of Queen's College, Oxford.

Crown 8vo. 7s. 6d.

THE STAR OF CHILDHOOD.

A First Book of Prayers and Instruction for Children.

Compiled by a Priest.

Edited by the Rev. T. T. Carter, M.A., Rector of Clewer, Berks.

With Illustrations. Royal 32mo. 2s. 6d.

THE DOCTRINE of RECONCILIATION TO GOD BY JESUS CHRIST.

Seven Lectures, preached during Lent, 1870, with a Prefatory Essay.

By W. H. Fremantle, M.A., Rector of St. Mary's, Bryanston Square.

Small 8vo. 2s.

PROGRESSIVE EXERCISES IN LATIN ELEGIAC VERSE.

By C. G. Gepp, B.A., late Junior Student of Christ Church, Oxford, and Assistant Master at Tonbridge School.

Second Edition, Revised. Crown 8vo. 3s. 6d.

SELF-RENUNCIATION.

From the French. With Introduction by the Rev. T. T. Carter, M.A., Rector of Clewer.

Crown 8vo. 6s.

LONDON, OXFORD, & CAMBRIDGE.

THE HIDDEN LIFE OF THE SOUL.

From the French. By the Author of 'A Dominican Artist,' 'Life of Madame Louise de France,' etc , etc.

Crown 8vo. 5s.

ANCIENT HYMNS

From the Roman Breviary. For Domestic Use every Morning and Evening of the Week, and on the Holy Days of the Church.

To which are added, Original Hymns, principally of Commemoration and Thanksgiving for Christ's Holy Ordinances.

By Richard Mant, D.D., sometime Lord Bishop of Down and Connor.

New Edition. Small 8vo. 5s.

THE TWO BROTHERS, *and other Poems.*

By Edward Henry Bickersteth, M.A., Author of 'Yesterday, To-day, and for Ever.'

Small 8vo. 6s.

A HISTORY of the Holy EASTERN CHURCH.

The Patriarchate of Antioch, to the Middle of the Fifth Century.

By the Rev. John Mason Neale, D.D., late Warden of Sackville College, East Grinsted.

Followed by a History of the Patriarchs of Antioch, translated from the Greek of Constantius I., Patriarch of Constantinople.

Edited, with an Introduction, by George Williams, B.D., Vicar of Ringwood, late Fellow of King's College, Cambridge.

8vo. [*In the Press.*

ESSAYS ON THE PLATONIC ETHICS.

By Thomas Maguire, LL.D. ex S.T.C.D., Professor of Latin, Queen's College, Galway.

8vo. 5s.

ST. JOHN CHRYSOSTOM'S LITURGY.

Translated by **H. C. Romanoff**, Author of 'Sketches of the Rites and
Customs of the Greco-Russian Church.'

With Illustrations. Square crown 8vo. 4s. 6d.

DEMOSTHENIS ORATIONES
PUBLICAE.

Edited by **G. H. Heslop**, M.A., late Fellow and Assistant Tutor
of Queen's College, Oxford; Head Master of St. Bees.

DE FALSÂ LEGATIONE. Forming a new Part of 'Catena Classicorum.'

Crown 8vo.   [*In the Press.*

DEMOSTHENIS ORATIONES
PRIVATAE.

Edited by the Rev. **Arthur Holmes**, M.A., Senior Fellow and Lecturer of Clare College, Cambridge; and Preacher at the
Chapel Royal, Whitehall.

DE CORONÂ. Forming a new Part of 'Catena Classicorum.'

Crown 8vo.   [*In the Press.*

THE LIFE OF JUSTIFICATION.

A Series of Lectures delivered in Substance at All Saints', Margaret
Street, in Lent, 1870.

By the Rev. **George Body**, B.A., Rector of Kirkby Misperton.

Crown 8vo. 4s. 6d.

THE ILIAD OF HOMER.

Translated by **J. G. Cordery**, late of Balliol College, Oxford, and
now of H.M. Bengal Civil Service.

Two vols. 8vo. 16s.

THE SAYINGS OF THE GREAT FORTY DAYS,

Between the Resurrection and Ascension, regarded as the Outlines of the Kingdom of God. In Five Discourses. With an Examination of Dr. Newman's Theory of Development.

By George Moberly, D.C.L., Bishop of Salisbury.

Fourth Edition. Uniform with Brighstone Sermons.
Crown 8vo. 7s. 6d.

DICTIONARY OF SECTS, HERESIES, AND SCHOOLS OF THOUGHT.

By Various Writers.

Edited by the Rev. **John Henry Blunt**, M.A., F.S.A.; Editor of 'The Annotated Book of Common Prayer.'

(FORMING THE SECOND PORTION OF THE 'SUMMARY. OF THEOLOGY AND ECCLESIASTICAL HISTORY,' WHICH MESSRS. RIVINGTON HAVE IN COURSE OF PREPARATION AS A 'THESAURUS THEOLOGICUS' FOR THE CLERGY AND LAITY OF THE CHURCH OF ENGLAND.)

Imperial 8vo.   [*In preparation.*

A PLAIN ACCOUNT OF THE ENGLISH BIBLE,

From the Earliest Times of its Translation to the Present Day.

By **John Henry Blunt**, M.A., Vicar of Kennington, Oxford; Editor of 'The Annotated Book of Common Prayer,' etc.

Crown 8vo. 3s. 6d.

The CHURCH of GOD and the BISHOPS:

An Essay suggested by the Convocation of the Vatican Council. By **Henry St. A. Von Liaño**. Authorized Translation.

Crown 8vo. 4s. 6d.

THE POPE AND THE COUNCIL.

By Janus. Authorized Translation from the German.
Third Edition, revised. Crown 8vo. 7s. 6d.

LETTERS FROM ROME on the COUNCIL.

By Quirinus. Reprinted from the *Allgemeine Zeitung.*
Authorized Translation.
Crown 8vo. 12s.

THE AMMERGAU PASSION PLAY.

Reprinted by permission from the *Times.* With some Introductory
Remarks on the Origin and Development of Miracle Plays,
and some Practical Hints for the use of Intending Visitors.

By the Rev. **Malcolm MacColl**, M.A., Chaplain to the Right Hon.
Lord Napier, K.T.

Fifth Edition. With a New Appendix, giving a continuous de-
scription of the Scenes and Tableaux of the Play, in the
order in which they take place. *Crown 8vo. 3s. 6d.*

The FIRST BOOK OF COMMON PRAYER OF EDWARD VI. AND THE ORDINAL OF 1549;

Together with the Order of the Communion, 1548.

Reprinted entire, and Edited by the Rev. **Henry Baskerville Walton**,
M.A., late Fellow and Tutor of Merton College.

With Introduction by the Rev. **Peter Goldsmith Medd**, M.A.,
Senior Fellow and Tutor of University College, Oxford.

Small 8vo. 6s.

THE PURSUIT OF HOLINESS.

A Sequel to 'Thoughts on Personal Religion,' intended to carry the
Reader somewhat farther onward in the Spiritual Life.

By **Edward Meyrick Goulburn**, D.D., Dean of Norwich.

Third Edition. Small 8vo. 5s.

LONDON, OXFORD, & CAMBRIDGE.

APOSTOLICAL SUCCESSION IN THE CHURCH OF ENGLAND.

By the Rev. Arthur W. Haddan, B.D., Rector of Barton-on-the-Heath, and late Fellow of Trinity College, Oxford.

8vo. 12s.

THE PRIEST TO THE ALTAR;

Or, Aids to the Devout Celebration of Holy Communion; chiefly after the Ancient Use of Sarum.

Second Edition. Enlarged, Revised, and Re-arranged with the Secretæ, Post-communion, etc., appended to the Collects, Epistles, and Gospels, throughout the Year.

8vo. 7s. 6d.

NEWMAN'S (J. H.) PAROCHIAL AND PLAIN SERMONS.

Edited by the Rev. W. J. Copeland, Rector of Farnham, Essex.

From the Text of the last Editions published by Messrs. Rivington.

Eight vols. Crown 8vo. 5s. each.

NEWMAN'S (J. H.) SERMONS, BEARING UPON SUBJECTS OF THE DAY.

Edited by the Rev. W. J. Copeland, Rector of Farnham, Essex.

From the Text of the last Edition published by Messrs. Rivington. With Index of Dates of all the Sermons.

Printed uniformly with the 'Parochial and Plain Sermons.'

Crown 8vo. 5s.

BRIGHSTONE SERMONS.

By George Moberly, D.C.L., Bishop of Salisbury.

Second Edition. Crown 8vo. 7s. 6d.

LONDON, OXFORD, & CAMBRIDGE.

The CHARACTERS of the OLD TESTAMENT.
In a Series of Sermons.

By the Rev. **Isaac Williams**, B.D., late Fellow of Trinity College, Oxford.

New Edition. Crown 8vo. 5s.

FEMALE CHARACTERS of HOLY SCRIPTURE.
In a Series of Sermons.

By the Rev. **Isaac Williams**, B.D., late Fellow of Trinity College, Oxford.

New Edition. Crown 8vo. 5s.

THE DIVINITY OF OUR LORD AND SAVIOUR JESUS CHRIST:
Being the Bampton Lectures for 1866.

By **Henry Parry Liddon**, D.D., D.C.L., Canon of St. Paul's, and Ireland Professor of Exegesis in the University of Oxford.

Fifth Edition. Crown 8vo. 5s.

SERMONS PREACHED BEFORE THE UNIVERSITY OF OXFORD.

By **Henry Parry Liddon**, D.D., D.C.L., Canon of St. Paul's, and Ireland Professor of Exegesis in the University of Oxford.

Fourth Edition. Crown 8vo. 5s.

A MANUAL FOR THE SICK;
With other Devotions.

By **Launcelot Andrewes**, D.D., sometime Lord Bishop of Winchester.

Edited, with a Preface, by **Henry Parry Liddon**, D.D., D.C.L., Canon of St. Paul's.

With Portrait. Second Edition. Large type. 24mo. 2s. 6d.

LONDON, OXFORD, & CAMBRIDGE.

10

WALTER KERR HAMILTON: BISHOP of SALISBURY.

A Sketch, Reprinted, with Additions and Corrections, from the *Guardian.*

By **Henry Parry Liddon**, D.D., D.C.L., Canon of St. Paul's.

Second Edition. 8vo. Limp cloth, 2s. 6d.

Or, bound with the Sermon, 'Life in Death,' 3s. 6d.

THE LIFE OF MADAME LOUISE DE FRANCE,

Daughter of Louis XV., also known as the Mother Térèse de S. Augustin. By the Author of 'A Dominican Artist,' etc.

Crown 8vo. 6s.

JOHN WESLEY'S PLACE IN CHURCH HISTORY DETERMINED,

With the aid of Facts and Documents unknown to, or unnoticed by, his Biographers.

With a New and Authentic Portrait.

By **R. Denny Urlin**, M.R.I.A., of the Middle Temple, Barrister-at-Law.

Small 8vo. 5s. 6d.

THE TREASURY OF DEVOTION:

A Manual of Prayers for General and Daily Use.

Compiled by a Priest. Edited by the Rev. **T. T. Carter**, M.A., Rector of Clewer, Berks.

Fourth Edition. 16mo, limp cloth 2s.; cloth extra, 2s. 6d.

Bound with the Book of Common Prayer, 3s. 6d.

LONDON, OXFORD, & CAMBRIDGE.

THE GUIDE TO HEAVEN:

A Book of Prayers for every Want. (For the Working Classes.)
Compiled by a Priest. Edited by the Rev. **T. T. Carter, M.A.**,
Rector of Clewer, Berks.

Second Edition. Crown 8vo, limp cloth, 1s. ; *cloth extra*, 1s. 6d.

A DOMINICAN ARTIST:

A Sketch of the Life of the Rev. Père Besson, of the Order of
St. Dominic.

By the Author of ' The Life of Madame Louise de France,' etc.

Crown 8vo. 9s.

THE REFORMATION OF THE CHURCH
OF ENGLAND;

Its History, Principles, and Results. A.D. 1514-1547.

By John **Henry Blunt**, M.A., Vicar of Kennington, Oxford, Editor
of ' The Annotated Book of Common Prayer,' Author of
' Directorium Pastorale,' etc., etc.

Second Edition. 8vo. 16s.

THE VIRGIN'S LAMP:

Prayers and Devout Exercises for English Sisters, chiefly composed
and selected by the late Rev. **J. M. Neale, D.D.**, Founder of
St. Margaret's, East Grinsted.

Small 8vo. 3s. 6d.

CATECHETICAL NOTES AND CLASS
QUESTIONS, LITERAL & MYSTICAL;

Chiefly on the Earlier Books of Holy Scripture.

By the late Rev. **J. M. Neale, D.D.**, Warden of Sackville College,
East Grinsted.

Crown 8vo. 5s.

SERMONS FOR CHILDREN:

Being Thirty-three short Readings, addressed to the Children of
St. Margaret's Home, East Grinsted.

By the late Rev. J. M. Neale, D.D., Warden of Sackville College.

Second Edition. Small 8vo. 3s. 6d.

THE WITNESS of the OLD TESTAMENT TO CHRIST.

The Boyle Lectures for the Year 1868.

By the Rev. Stanley Leathes, M.A., Professor of Hebrew in King's
College, London, and Minister of St. Philip's, Regent Street.

8vo. 9s.

THE WITNESS of ST. PAUL to CHRIST:

Being the Boyle Lectures for 1869.

With an Appendix, on the Credibility of the Acts, in Reply to
the Recent Strictures of Dr. Davidson.

By the Rev. Stanley Leathes, M.A., Professor of Hebrew in King's
College, London, and Minister of St. Philip's, Regent Street.

8vo. 10s. 6d.

HONORÉ DE BALZAC.

Edited, with English Notes and Introductory Notice, by Henri Van
Laun, formerly French Master at Cheltenham College, and
now Master of the French Language and Literature at
the Edinburgh Academy.

(BEING THE FIRST VOLUME OF 'SELECTIONS FROM MODERN FRENCH AUTHORS.')

Crown 8vo. 3s. 6d.

H. A. TAINE.

Edited, with English Notes and Introductory Notice, by Henri Van Laun, formerly French Master at Cheltenham College, and now Master of the French Language and Literature at the Edinburgh Academy.

(BEING THE SECOND VOLUME OF 'SELECTIONS FROM MODERN FRENCH AUTHORS.')

Crown 8vo.   3s. 6d.

DEAN ALFORD'S GREEK TESTAMENT.

With English Notes, intended for the Upper Forms of Schools, and for Pass-men at the Universities.

Abridged by Bradley H. Alford, M.A., late Scholar of Trinity College, Cambridge.

Crown 8vo.   10s. 6d.

ELEMENTARY ALGEBRA.

By J. Hamblin Smith, M.A, Gonville and Caius College, and Lecturer at St. Peter's College, Cambridge.

New Edition, Revised and Enlarged.   Crown 8vo.   4s. 6d.

ELEMENTARY TRIGONOMETRY.

By J. Hamblin Smith, M.A., Gonville and Caius College, and Lecturer at St. Peter's College, Cambridge.

New Edition, Revised and Enlarged.   Crown 8vo.   4s. 6d.

ELEMENTARY STATICS.

By J. Hamblin Smith, M.A., Gonville and Caius College, and Lecturer at St. Peter's College, Cambridge.

New Edition, Revised and Enlarged.   [In the Press.

ELEMENTARY HYDROSTATICS.

By J. Hamblin Smith, M.A., Gonville and Caius College, and
Lecturer at St. Peter's College, Cambridge.

New Edition, Revised and Enlarged. Crown 8vo. 3s.

EXERCISES ADAPTED TO ALGEBRA.

PART I.

By J. Hamblin Smith, M.A., Gonville and Caius College; and
Lecturer at St. Peter's College, Cambridge.

Crown 8vo. 2s, 6d.

Copies may be had without the Answers.

ELEMENTS OF GEOMETRY.

Part I., containing the first Two Books of Euclid, with Exercises and
Notes, arranged with the Abbreviations admitted in
the Cambridge Examinations.

By J. Hamblin Smith, M.A., Gonville and Caius College; and
Lecturer at St. Peter's College, Cambridge.

Crown 8vo. 1s. 6d.; cloth, 2s.

ARITHMETIC, THEORETICAL AND PRACTICAL.

By W. H. Girdlestone, M.A., of Christ's College, Cambridge,
Principal of the Theological College, Gloucester.

New and Revised Edition. Crown 8vo. 6s. 6d.

Also an Edition for Schools. *Small 8vo. 3s. 6d.*

CLASSICAL EXAMINATION PAPERS.

Edited, with Notes and References, by **P. J. F. Gantillon, M.A.**,
sometime Scholar of St. John's College, Cambridge;
Classical Master in Cheltenham College.

*Crown 8vo. 7s. 6d. Or interleaved with writing-paper for Notes,
half-bound, 10s. 6d.*

LONDON, OXFORD, & CAMBRIDGE.

THE STORY OF THE GOSPELS.

In a single Narrative, combined from the Four Evangelists, showing in a new translation their unity. To which is added, a like continuous narrative in the Original Greek.

By the Rev. **William Pound**, M.A., late Fellow of St. John's College, Cambridge; Principal of Appulddurcombe School, Isle of Wight.

Two vols. 8vo. 36s.

THE LYRICS OF HORACE,

Done into English Rhyme.

By **Thomas Charles Baring**, M.A., late Fellow of Brasenose College, Oxford.

Small 4to. 7s.

A PLAIN AND SHORT HISTORY OF ENGLAND FOR CHILDREN,

In Letters from a Father to his Son. With a Set of Questions at the end of each Letter.

By **George Davys**, D.D., late Bishop of Peterborough.

New Edition, with Twelve Coloured Illustrations.

Square Crown 8vo. 3s. 6d.

A Cheap Edition for Schools, with portrait of Edward VI.

18mo. 1s. 6d.

HISTORY OF THE COLLEGE OF ST. JOHN THE EVANGELIST, CAMBRIDGE.

By **Thomas Baker**, B.D., Ejected Fellow.

Edited for the Syndics of the University Press, by **John E. B. Mayor**, M.A., Fellow of St. John's College.

Two vols. 8vo. 24s.

LONDON, OXFORD, & CAMBRIDGE.

HELP AND COMFORT FOR THE SICK POOR.

By the Author of ' Sickness; its Trials and Blessings.'

New Edition. Small 8vo. 1s.

THE DOGMATIC FAITH:

An Inquiry into the relation subsisting between Revelation and Dogma. Being the Bampton Lectures for 1867.

By **Edward Garbett, M.A.**, Incumbent of Christ Church, Surbiton.

Second Edition. Crown 8vo. 5s.

SKETCHES OF THE RITES & CUSTOMS OF THE GRECO-RUSSIAN CHURCH.

By **H. C. Romanoff.** With an Introductory Notice by the Author of ' The Heir of Redclyffe.'

' Second Edition. Crown 8vo. 7s. 6d.

HOUSEHOLD THEOLOGY:

A Handbook of Religious Information respecting the Holy Bible, the Prayer Book, the Church, the Ministry, Divine Worship, the Creeds, etc., etc.

By **John Henry Blunt, M.A.**

New Edition. Small 8vo. 3s. 6d.

CURIOUS MYTHS OF THE MIDDLE AGES.

By **S. Baring-Gould, M.A.**, Author of ' Post-Mediæval Preachers,' etc. With Illustrations.

Complete in one Volume.

New Edition. Crown 8vo. 6s.

LONDON, OXFORD, & CAMBRIDGE.

MEMOIR OF THE RIGHT REV. JOHN

STRACHAN, D.D., LL.D., *First Bishop of Toronto.*

By **A. N. Bethune**, D.D., D.C.L., his Successor in the See.

8vo. 10*s.*

THE PRAYER BOOK INTERLEAVED;

With Historical Illustrations and Explanatory Notes arranged
parallel to the Text.

By the Rev. **W. M. Campion**, D.D., Fellow and Tutor of Queen's
College, and Rector of St. Botolph's, and the Rev. **W. J. Beamont**,
M.A., late Fellow of Trinity College, Cambridge.

With a Preface by the Lord Bishop of Ely.

Fifth Edition. Small 8vo. 7*s.* 6*d.*

CONSOLING THOUGHTS IN SICKNESS.

Edited by **Henry Bailey**, B.D., Warden of St. Augustine's College,
Canterbury.

Large type. Fine Edition. Small 8vo. 2*s.* 6*d.*

Also a Cheap Edition, 1*s.* 6*d.*; or in paper cover, 1*s.*

SICKNESS; ITS TRIALS & BLESSINGS.

New Edition, Small 8vo. 3*s.* 6*d.*

Also a Cheap Edition, 1*s.* 6*d.*; or in paper cover, 1*s.*

HYMNS AND POEMS FOR THE SICK
AND SUFFERING;

In connection with the Service for the Visitation of the Sick.
Selected from various Authors.

Edited by **T. V. Fosbery**, M.A., Vicar of St. Giles's, Reading.

New Edition. Small 8vo. 3*s.* 6*d.*

LONDON, OXFORD, & CAMBRIDGE.

SOI-MÊME; a Story of a Wilful Life.

Small 8vo.   3s. 6d.

· THE HAPPINESS OF THE BLESSED,

Considered as to the Particulars of their State: their Recognition
of each other in that State: and its Differences of Degrees.

To which are added, Musings on the Church and her Services.

By Richard Mant, D.D., sometime Lord Bishop of Down & Connor.

New Edition.   Small 8vo.   3s. 6d.

THE HOLY BIBLE.

With Notes and Introductions.

By Chr. Wordsworth, D.D., Bishop of Lincoln.

Second Edition.   Imperial 8vo.

Vol.   I.   Genesis to Deuteronomy.   38s.
Vol.   II.   Joshua to Samuel.   21s.
Vol.   III.   Kings to Esther.   21s.
Vol.   IV.   Job to Song of Solomon.   34s.
Vol.   V.   Isaiah to Ezekiel.   32s. 6d.
Vol.   VI.   Daniel.   6s.
               The Minor Prophets.   12s.

THE MACCABEES AND THE CHURCH;

Or the History of the Maccabees Considered with Reference to the
Present Condition and Prospects of the Church.

Two Sermons preached before the University of Cambridge.

By Chr. Wordsworth, D.D., Bishop of Lincoln.

Crown 8vo.   2s. 6d.

MISCELLANEOUS POEMS.

By **Henry Francis Lyte**, M.A.

New Edition.   Small 8vo.   5s.

PERRANZABULOE, THE LOST CHURCH
FOUND;

Or, The Church of England not a New Church, but Ancient, Apostolical, and Independent, and a Protesting Church Nine Hundred Years before the Reformation.

By the Rev. **C. T. Collins Trelawny**, M.A., formerly Rector of Timsbury, Somerset, and late Fellow of Balliol College, Oxford.

With Illustrations.   New Edition.   Crown 8vo.   3s. 6d.

CATECHESIS; *or,* CHRISTIAN INSTRUCTION

Preparatory to Confirmation and First Communion.

By **Charles Wordsworth**, D.C.L., Bishop of St. Andrew's.

New Edition.   Small 8vo.   2s.

WARNINGS OF THE HOLY WEEK, *etc.;*

Being a Course of Parochial Lectures for the Week before Easter and the Easter Festivals.

By the Rev. **W. Adams**, M.A., late Vicar of St. Peter's-in-the-East, Oxford, and Fellow of Merton College.

Sixth Edition.   Small 8vo.   4s. 6d.

CONSOLATIO; *or,* COMFORT FOR THE
AFFLICTED.

Edited by the Rev. **C. E. Kennaway**. With a Preface by Samuel Wilberforce, D.D., Lord Bishop of Winchester.

New Edition.   Small 8vo.   3s. 6d.

LONDON, OXFORD, & CAMBRIDGE.

THE HILLFORD CONFIRMATION: a Tale.

By M. C. Phillpotts.

New Edition. 18mo. 1s.

FROM MORNING TO EVENING:

A Book for Invalids.

From the French of M. L'Abbé Henri Perreyve.
Translated and adapted by an Associate of the Sisterhood of
S. John Baptist, Clewer.

Crown 8vo. 5s.

FAMILY PRAYERS;

Compiled from Various Sources (chiefly from Bishop Hamilton's
Manual), and arranged on the Liturgical Principle.

By Edward Meyrick Goulburn, D.D., Dean of Norwich.

New Edition. Crown 8vo, large type, 3s. 6d.

Cheap Edition. 16mo. 1s.

THE ANNUAL REGISTER:

A Review of Public Events at Home and Abroad, for the Year 1870;
being the Eighth Volume of an Improved Series.

8vo. 18s.

*** *The Volumes for* 1863 *to* 1869 *may be had, price* 18s. *each.*

A PROSE TRANSLATION OF VIRGIL'S ECLOGUES AND GEORGICS

By an Oxford Graduate.

Crown 8vo. 2s. 6d.

LONDON, OXFORD, & CAMBRIDGE.

THE CAMBRIDGE PARAGRAPH BIBLE
OF THE AUTHORIZED ENGLISH VERSION.

With the Text Revised by a Collation of its Early and other
Principal Editions, the Use of the Italic type made Uniform,
the Marginal References Re-modelled, and a Critical
Introduction prefixed.

By the Rev. **F. H. Scrivener**, M.A., Rector of St. Gerrans; Editor
of the Greek Testament, Codex Augiensis, etc. Edited
for the Syndics of the University Press

Crown 4to.

Part I., Genesis to Solomon's Song, 15s.

Part II., Apocrypha and New Testament, 15s.

To be completed in Three Parts.

Part III., Prophetical Books, will be ready during 1871.

*** A small number of copies has also been printed, on *good
writing paper*, with one column of print and wide margin to
each page for MS. notes. *Part I, 20s.; Part II, 20s.*

QUIET MOMENTS:

A Four Weeks' Course of Thoughts and Meditations,
before Evening Prayer and at Sunset.

By Lady Charlotte Maria Pepys.

New Edition. Small 8vo. 2s. 6d.

MORNING NOTES OF PRAISE:
A Series of Meditations upon the Morning Psalms.

By Lady Charlotte Maria Pepys.

New Edition. Small 8vo. 2s. 6d.

LONDON, OXFORD, & CAMBRIDGE.

22

YESTERDAY, TO-DAY, AND FOR EVER;
A Poem in Twelve Books.

By Edward Henry Bickersteth, M.A., Vicar of Christ Church, Hampstead, and Chaplain to the Bishop of Ripon.

Fifth Edition. *Small 8vo.* *6s.*

THE COMMENTARIES OF GAIUS:

Translated, with Notes, by **J. T. Abdy**, LL.D., Regius Professor of Laws in the University of Cambridge, and Barrister-at-Law of the Norfolk Circuit: formerly Fellow of Trinity Hall; and **Bryan Walker**, M.A., M.L.; Fellow and Lecturer of Corpus Christi College, and Law Lecturer of St. John's College, Cambridge; formerly Law Student of Trinity Hall and Chancellor's Legal Medallist.

Crown 8vo. *12s. 6d.*

SACRED ALLEGORIES:

The Shadow of the Cross—The Distant Hills—The Old Man's Home—The King's Messengers.

By the Rev. **W. Adams**, M.A., late Fellow of Merton College, Oxford.

Presentation Edition. With Engravings from original designs by Charles W. Cope, R.A., John C. Horsley, A.R.A., Samuel Palmer, Birket Foster, and George Hicks.

Small 4to. *10s. 6d.*

The Four Allegories, separately. *Crown 8vo.* *2s. 6d. each.*

HERBERT TRESHAM:
A Tale of the Great Rebellion.

By the late Rev. **J. M. Neale**, D.D., sometime Scholar of Trinity College, Cambridge, and late Warden of Sackville College, East Grinsted.

New Edition. *Small 8vo.* *3s. 6d.*

THE MANOR FARM: a Tale.

By **M. C. Phillpotts**, Author of 'The Hillford Confirmation.'

With Four Illustrations. *Small 8vo.* *3s. 6d.*

LIBER PRECUM PUBLICARUM
ECCLESIÆ ANGLICANÆ,

A Gulielmo Bright, A.M., et Petro Goldsmith Medd, A.M.,
Presbyteris, Collegii Universitatis in Acad. Oxon.
Sociis, Latine redditus.

New Edition, with all the Rubrics in red. Small 8vo. 6s.

BIBLE READINGS FOR FAMILY PRAYER.

By the Rev. **W. H. Ridley,** M.A., Rector of Hambleden.

Crown 8vo.

Old Testament—Genesis and Exodus. 2s.

New Testament, 3s. 6d. { St. Matthew and St. Mark. 2s.
{ St. Luke and St. John. 2s.

INSTRUCTIONS FOR THE USE OF
CANDIDATES FOR HOLY ORDERS,

And of the Parochial Clergy; with Acts of Parliament relating to
the same, and Forms proposed to be used.

By **Christopher Hodgson,** M.A., Secretary to the Governors of
Queen Anne's Bounty.

Ninth Edition, Revised and Enlarged, 8vo. 16s.

ENGLAND RENDERED IMPREGNABLE

By the practical Military Organization and efficient Equipment of her
National Forces; and her Present Position, Armament, Coast
Defences, Administration, and Future Power considered.

By **H. A. L.,** 'The Old Shekarry.'

8vo. With Illustrations. 21s.

WHO IS RESPONSIBLE FOR THE WAR?

By Scrutator.

With an Appendix, containing Four Letters, reprinted
(by permission) from the *Times*.

Second Edition. Crown 8vo. 6s.

AN OUTLINE OF LOGIC.

For the Use of Teachers and Students.

By the Rev. **Francis Garden**, M.A., Trinity College, Cambridge;
Sub-Dean of Her Majesty's Chapels Royal, Chaplain to the House-
hold in St. James's Palace, and Professor of Mental and
Moral Science, Queen's College, London.

Second Edition. Small 8vo. 4s.

THE LAST THREE BISHOPS,

Appointed by the Crown for the Anglican Church of Canada.

By **Fennings Taylor**, Deputy Clerk of the Senate of Canada.

Second Edition. With Portraits. Small 4to. 10s. 6d.

COMMENTARY on the BOOK OF ISAIAH,

Critical, Historical, and Prophetical;

Including a Revised English Translation, with Introduction and
Appendices on the Nature of Scripture Prophecy, the Life and
Times of Isaiah, the Genuineness of the later Prophecies, the
Structure and History of the whole Book, the Assyrian History
in Isaiah's Days, and Various Difficult Passages.

By the Rev. **T. R. Birks**, Vicar of Holy Trinity, Cambridge.

8vo. 12s.

LONDON, OXFORD, & CAMBRIDGE.

CATENA CLASSICORUM:

A SERIES OF CLASSICAL AUTHORS,

EDITED BY MEMBERS OF BOTH UNIVERSITIES UNDER THE DIRECTION OF

THE REV. ARTHUR HOLMES, M.A.,

Senior Fellow and Lecturer of Clare College, Cambridge, and Preacher at the Chapel Royal, Whitehall.

AND

THE REV. CHARLES BIGG, M.A.,

Late Senior Student and Tutor of Christ Church, Oxford, Second Classical Master of Cheltenham College.

Crown 8vo.

THE FOLLOWING PARTS HAVE BEEN ALREADY PUBLISHED :—

SOPHOCLIS TRAGOEDIAE.

Edited by R. C. JEBB, M.A., Fellow and Assistant Tutor of Trinity College, Cambridge, and Public Orator of the University,
The Electra, 3*s.* 6*d.*   The Ajax, 3*s.* 6*d.*

JUVENALIS SATIRAE.

Edited by G. A. SIMCOX, M.A., Fellow and Classical Lecturer of Queen's College, Oxford.
3*s.* 6*d.*

THUCYDIDIS HISTORIA.

Edited by CHARLES BIGG, M.A, late Senior Student and Tutor of Christ Church, Oxford. Second Classical Master of Cheltenham College.
Books I. and II. with Introductions.   6*s.*

LONDON, OXFORD, & CAMBRIDGE.

DEMOSTHENIS ORATIONES PUBLICAE.

Edited by G. H. HESLOP, M.A., Late Fellow and Assistant Tutor of Queen's College, Oxford. Head Master of St. Bees.

The Olynthiacs. 2s. 6d.

The Philippics. 3s.

ARISTOPHANIS COMOEDIAE.

Edited by W. C. GREEN, M.A., late Fellow of King's College, Cambridge; Assistant Master at Rugby School.

The Acharnians and the Knights. 4s.

The Clouds. 3s. 6d.

The Wasps. 3s. 6d.

An Edition of the Acharnians and the Knights, Revised and especially adapted for Use in Schools. 4s.

ISOCRATIS ORATIONES.

Edited by JOHN EDWIN SANDYS, M.A., Fellow and Tutor of St. John's College, and Classical Lecturer at Jesus College, Cambridge.

Ad Demonicum et Panegyricus. 4s. 6d.

PERSII SATIRAE.

Edited by A. PRETOR, M.A., of Trinity College, Cambridge. Classical Lecturer of Trinity Hall. 3s. 6d.

HOMERI ILIAS.

Edited by S. H. REYNOLDS, M.A., Fellow and Tutor of Brasenose College, Oxford.

Books I. to XII. 6s.

TERENTI COMOEDIAE.

Edited by T. L. PAPILLON, M.A., Fellow of New College, Oxford, and late Fellow of Merton.

Andria et Eunuchus. 4s. 6d.

KEYS TO CHRISTIAN KNOWLEDGE.

Small 8vo.   2s. 6d. each.

A KEY TO THE KNOWLEDGE AND USE OF THE BOOK OF COMMON PRAYER.

By **John Henry Blunt,** M.A.

A KEY TO THE KNOWLEDGE AND USE OF THE HOLY BIBLE.

By **John Henry Blunt,** M.A.

A KEY TO THE KNOWLEDGE OF CHURCH HISTORY (ANCIENT).

Edited by **John Henry Blunt,** M.A.

A KEY TO THE NARRATIVE OF THE FOUR GOSPELS.

By **John Pilkington Norris,** M.A., Canon of Bristol, formerly one of Her Majesty's Inspectors of Schools.

A KEY TO CHRISTIAN DOCTRINE & PRACTICE.

(Founded on the Church Catechism.)
By **John Henry Blunt,** M.A.

A KEY TO THE NARRATIVE OF THE ACTS OF THE APOSTLES.

By **John Pilkington Norris,** M.A., Canon of Bristol, formerly one of Her Majesty's Inspectors of Schools.

LONDON, OXFORD, & CAMBRIDGE.

THE 'ASCETIC LIBRARY:'

A Series of Translations of Spiritual Works for Devotional
Reading from Catholic Sources.

Edited by the Rev. Orby Shipley, M.A.

Square Crown 8vo.

THE MYSTERIES OF MOUNT CALVARY.

Translated from the Latin of Antonio de Guevara. 3*s*, 6*d*.

PREPARATION FOR DEATH.

Translated from the Italian of Alfonso, Bishop of S. Agatha. 5*s*.

COUNSELS ON HOLINESS OF LIFE.

Translated from the Spanish of 'The Sinner's Guide' by
Luis de Granada. 5*s*.

EXAMINATION OF CONSCIENCE UPON SPECIAL SUBJECTS.

Translated and Abridged from the French of Tronson. 5*s*.

RIVINGTON'S DEVOTIONAL SERIES,

Elegantly printed with red borders. 16mo. 2s 6d.

THOMAS À KEMPIS, OF THE IMITATION OF CHRIST.

Also a cheap Edition, without the red borders, 1s., or in Cover, 6d.

THE RULE AND EXERCISES OF HOLY LIVING.

By **Jeremy Taylor**, D.D., Bishop of Down, and Connor, and Dromore.

Also a cheap Edition, without the red borders, 1s.

THE RULE AND EXERCISES OF HOLY DYING.

By **Jeremy Taylor**, D,D,, Bishop of Down, and Connor, and Dromore,

Also a cheap Edition, without the red borders, 1s,

₊ The 'Holy Living' and the 'Holy Dying' may be had bound together in One Volume, 5s., or without the red borders, 2s. 6d.

A SHORT AND PLAIN INSTRUCTION

For the better Understanding of the Lord's Supper; to which is annexed, the Office of the Holy Communion, with proper Helps and Directions.

By **Thomas Wilson**, D.D., late Lord Bishop of Sodor and Man.

Complete Edition, in large type.

Also a cheap Edition, without the red borders, 1s., or in Cover, 6d.

INTRODUCTION TO THE DEVOUT LIFE.

From the French of St. Francis of Sales, Bishop and Prince of Geneva. A New Translation.

A PRACTICAL TREATISE CONCERNING EVIL THOUGHTS.

By **William Chilcot**, M.A.

ENGLISH POEMS AND PROVERBS.

By **George Herbert**.

LONDON, OXFORD, & CAMBRIDGE.

NEW PAMPHLETS.

BY THE RIGHT HON. SIR ROBERT PHILLIMORE, D.C.L.

JUDGMENT,

Delivered by The Right Hon. Sir Robert Phillimore, D.C.L., Official Principal of the Arches Court of Canterbury, in the case of the Office of the Judge promoted by Sheppard *v.* Bennett. Edited by WALTER G. F. PHILLIMORE, B.C.L., of the Middle Temple, Barrister-at-Law; Fellow of All Souls' College, and Vinerian Scholar, Oxford.

Small 8vo. Cheap Edition. 1s.

BY CANON LIDDON.

ST. PAUL'S AND LONDON:

A Sermon, preached at St. Paul's Cathedral, on the Fourth Sunday after Epiphany, 1871.

8vo. 6d.

THE DAY OF WORK:

A Sermon, preached in St. Paul's Cathedral on Sunday, August 6th, 1871; being the Morrow of the Funeral of the Very Rev. H. L. Mansel, D.D., Dean of St. Paul's.

8vo. 1s.

BY ARCHDEACON BICKERSTETH.

A CHARGE,

Prepared for delivery at his Twelfth Visitation of the Archdeaconry of Buckingham, in June, 1871.

8vo. 1s.

BY ARCHDEACON DENISON.

THE THREE POLICIES:

A Letter to the Lord Bishop of Gloucester and Bristol.

Second Edition, with Postscript. 8vo. 1s.

LONDON, OXFORD, & CAMBRIDGE.

Eight Volumes, Crown 8vo, 5s. each.

A New and Uniform Edition of

A DEVOTIONAL COMMENTARY.
ON THE
GOSPEL NARRATIVE.

BY THE

REV. ISAAC WILLIAMS, B.D.

FORMERLY FELLOW OF TRINITY COLLEGE, OXFORD.

—*oo*—

THOUGHTS ON THE STUDY OF THE HOLY GOSPELS.

Characteristic Differences in the Four Gospels—Our Lord's Manifestations of Himself—The Rule of Scriptural Interpretation Furnished by Our Lord—Analogies of the Gospel—Mention of Angels in the Gospels—Places of Our Lord's Abode and Ministry—Our Lord's Mode of Dealing with His Apostles—Conclusion.

A HARMONY OF THE FOUR EVANGELISTS.

Our Lord's Nativity—Our Lord's Ministry (Second Year)—Our Lord's Ministry (Third Year)—The Holy Week—Our Lord's Passion—Our Lord's Resurrection.

OUR LORD'S NATIVITY.

The Birth at Bethlehem—The Baptism in Jordan—The First Passover.

OUR LORD'S MINISTRY. SECOND YEAR.

The Second Passover—Christ with the Twelve—The Twelve sent Forth.

OUR LORD'S MINISTRY. THIRD YEAR.

Teaching in Galilee—Teaching at Jerusalem—Last Journey from Galilee to Jerusalem.

THE HOLY WEEK.

The Approach to Jerusalem—The Teaching in the Temple—The Discourse on the Mount of Olives—The Last Supper.

OUR LORD'S PASSION.

The Hour of Darkness—The Agony—The Apprehension—The Condemnation—The Day of Sorrows—The Hall of Judgment—The Crucifixion—The Sepulture.

OUR LORD'S RESURRECTION.

The Day of Days—The Grave Visited—Christ Appearing—The Going to Emmaus—The Forty Days—The Apostles Assembled—The Lake in Galilee—The Mountain in Galilee—The Return from Galilee.

LONDON, OXFORD, & CAMBRIDGE.

CPSIA information can be obtained
at www.ICGtesting.com
Printed in the USA
BVHW042139300920
590056BV00005B/347